# the word on business

2

# jenny luesby

# the word on business

## it's an information economy.
## be a smart informer.

FINANCIAL TIMES
Prentice Hall

*An imprint of* **Pearson Education**
London / New York / San Francisco / Toronto / Sydney / Tokyo / Singapore
Hong Kong / Cape Town / Madrid / Paris / Milan / Munich / Amsterdam

PEARSON EDUCATION LIMITED

Head Office:
Edinburgh Gate
Harlow CM20 2JE
Tel: +44 (0)1279 623623
Fax: +44 (0)1279 431059

London Office:
128 Long Acre, London WC2E 9AN
Tel: +44 (0)20 7447 2000
Fax: +44 (0)20 7240 5771
Website: www.business-minds.com

---

First published in Great Britain in 2001

ISBN 0 273 64411 4

British Library Cataloguing in Publication Data
A CIP catalogue record for this book can be obtained from the British Library.

This publication is designed to provide accurate and authoritative information in regard
to the subject matter covered. It is sold with the understanding that neither the author nor
the publisher is engaged in rendering legal, investing, or any other professional service.
If legal advice or other expert assistance is required, the service of a competent
professional person should be sought.

The publisher and contributors make no representation, express or implied, with regard
to the accuracy of the information contained in this book and cannot accept any
responsibility or liability for any errors or omissions that it may contain.

10 9 8 7 6 5 4 3 2 1

Typeset by Northern Phototypesetting Co. Ltd, Bolton
Printed and bound in Great Britain by Bell & Bain Ltd, Glasgow

*The Publishers' policy is to use paper manufactured from sustainable forests.*

# About the author

**Jenny Luesby** has been writing about business, finance and economics since 1982. Before joining the *Financial Times*, she was a report writer, first for the Economist Intelligence Unit and then for the BBC World Service. At the *FT*, she worked as both an editor and writer, and from 1994 was industry correspondent for the world's second largest industry, chemicals. Commended in the 1996 Industrial Journalism Awards for Scoop of the Year, Jenny has worked extensively as a trainer of journalists, for the British Council, the Thomson Foundation, the KnowHow Fund, and numerous journalism schools and institutes. In 1998 she left the *FT* to start her own business: a residential training centre in the south of France.

For information about Jenny Luesby's current programme of one-week residential courses, and customised on-site training, please see www.business-minds.com

*To Ena Freeman*
*and*
*Len Freeman*

# Contents

# Preface

We all read about business sometimes – maybe just occasionally, but often as a matter of course. We do it to short-cut experience – to find out what's going on so that we can make smarter decisions. But so much of what's written about business is arcane, irrelevant and impenetrable. We have to be really dedicated to get what we want, and mostly we don't have the time.

It's a problem this book seeks to address. I wrote it because every time I went to teach people about business writing they asked for a book: and there wasn't one. Not something that made sense of the whole business information agenda from why to how.

The sum is a text for anyone who puts together business information for the public – as news, website content, or in any other form meant for outsiders. It's about giving readers what they want, and what they will come back for. This makes it more than a manual for writers. Business news starts within business. Companies that understand the needs of audiences, and of the information machine that serves them, inform differently and even behave differently.

Perhaps more important still, readers need this information. We live in a world where politics has shifted seismically away from the nation state as carer, transforming business information into lifeblood for a global labour force now responsible for its own successes.

This role is one the news industry is only just beginning to explore. But as business informers develop, readers are getting smarter, quicker. And that's doing something to economies. The difference between a first-time employer, mortgage-seeker, supplies-buyer, investor or whatever, and a third timer at anything is greater speed, efficiency and productivity. Pre-informed, even the first timer moves well.

We've all heard plenty about knowledge as power. But knowledge as an economic miracle is an idea we've yet fully to absorb. This isn't just a story about knowledge workers. It's a future built by knowledgeable workers and knowledgeable businesses based on trillions of words on business.

That said, you don't have to buy the idea that you're part of an unfolding economic revolution. If you just want to write copy that scores the best of hit-rates and triggers clamours for more, this is a book to set you on your way. It will give you the skills to send back engaging and rewarding news from the frontiers of business.

And for those of you in business, rather than writing about it, this is your wake-up call on the information age: an insight into what's going to be required of you, and why.

*Jenny Luesby*

# Acknowledgements

I should like, above all, to thank Ross Tieman, Jo Lazarus and Robert Tobin for their support, encouragement and insights during the many months that I spent writing this book. Also my thanks go to Clive Cookson, Dick and Christina Holttum, Peggy Hollinger, Susie Jambor, Harriet Martin, Nick Boisseau, Vanessa Houlder, Jonathan Prynn and Wendy Hudlass for their interest and feedback, to Emma Lazarus for her research into entrepreneurs, to Graham Watts for starting me out on the road to teaching, and to my publisher Richard Stagg for seeing a better book than I had thought of when I found him.

**'How will the change strike me and you?'**

Robert Browning

# 1

# A newborn power

## ▶ The power of the word

In the twenty-first century, the difference between rich and poor, success and failure, is knowledge, which doesn't mean that a command of medieval literature, KiSwahili or even metaphysics is going to keep you above the poverty line. The knowledge that counts now is the new literacy – financial literacy.

As each year passes, understanding business and finance is marking the divide for more and more of us. For most of the world's population, it's now so basic to our choices, our welfare and our livelihoods that it's already carving a line between the haves and the have-nots.

> **In the twenty-first century, the difference between rich and poor, success and failure, is knowledge.**

But it's not like the old kind of literacy, which served its purpose if you learnt it from a dictionary and applied it whenever necessary. Financial understanding on its own doesn't end missed opportunities and undesired burdens. You can be flattened by a collapse in the housing market just as completely even when you understand what drives house prices. To be truly financially literate means knowing what's happening.

Just try it for yourself. You may understand how a compound interest rate is constructed, but is 4 per cent good, bad or indifferent? You may know what a rights issue is, but does that mean you should exercise the one you've just been allocated? You may be clear that exports are the way to grow if you're operating in a stagnant economy, but does that tell you which market to go after?

Financial literacy is only literacy when it combines a knowledge of principles with a knowledge of the state of play – and that takes business news. News, that is, in the sense of information about commerce, finance or economies put together for outside audiences.

> Financial literacy is only literacy when it combines a knowledge of principles with a knowledge of the state of play.

The core of this book is a practical manual offering the skills to research and present business news so that it delivers financial literacy. As such, it's as applicable to corporate websites and research reports as it is to business newspapers, broadcast media and press releases. But its value begins with an assault on your mindset. Until you can see where your news fits into the financial literacy spectrum, you won't be writing anything that anyone wants to read. Because – heresy – business news can be boring, confusing or just spun puff. And it's need that sifts the best from the rest.

It's clear there is a need. Every day we put out reams of press releases, print thousands of business news pages and broadcast millions of words on business through internet news services, e-zines, intranets, electronic news groups, television, radio, newspapers and trade journals. In addition, there are more than two million corporate websites and legions of market research and consultancy companies specializing in business information. And the information gets read. Millions of people are reading business news, and millions of people are applying what they learn.

Yet there aren't too many theorists looking at what all those readers are getting from the news. In the vanguard, there are academics assessing the impact on personal welfare of information disadvantage. And the conclusions are clear: the well-informed secure better outcomes (see box opposite).

But no one has yet multiplied that equation to reach the startling but obvious conclusion that the quantity and quality of business news has a profound impact on economic growth. As more and more of us are steered away from lame ducks, warned of impending shortages or gluts and directed to the ways and places where the returns are best, the overall effect is greater efficiency. This is structural adjustment – as we all head for the activities where we have the most advantage and can create the most wealth – as it was always meant to be. So why should you care? Because once you've logged this, your content will change. You will write differently, about different things: and the readers will come.

Take Asia. You may think big economics is a domain a long way from yours. But if business news – across its entire breadth – had kept pace with the region's shift from investment opportunity to sated market, there would have been no crash: just a gentle slowdown in new money. Some market research here, a clutch of newspaper articles there, a corporate website, an e-zine and a radio feature that offered some insight into the approach of equilibrium in the region's manufacturing industry: taken together these would have prevented a human disaster.

> ## The information dream
>
> 'An advanced information infrastructure will enable US firms to compete and win in the global economy, generating good jobs for the American people and economic growth for the nation … Information is one of the nation's most critical economic resources, for service industries as well as manufacturing, for economic as well as national security.'
>
> Source: The White House 1993

More than that, when the sum of our knowledge was a gold-rush mentality, anything that helped us fill out the picture would have been appreciated. And when readers feel wiser and smarter after reading something, they go back for more. They also act on this new insight.

If you doubt that, take a look at your own livelihood. It's possible you don't use, won't use and never have used business information. Your pension (chosen for you) is just fine, your bank balance too. You have no mortgage and no need to invest. You don't anticipate big bills for school fees or weddings. You have a job that is secure for your lifetime. Your company will always keep growing. The future of your industry is assured and your skills will always be wanted, just as they are, just where they are. And all that by happenstance!

**When readers feel wiser and smarter after reading something, they go back for more.**

It's more likely, however, that you read things that helped you get where you are (think about it) and that there's more out there which will take you further still. And when you spot the new signposts, you'll act on them.

It is this reality that is making business news the Information Age service, above all others, that is transforming our lives and our economies. By guiding us to greater gains, it is emerging as a visible hand in the new economy: matching markets, directing growth and delivering advantage to anyone who chooses to act on it – that is, of course, providing the news is the stuff of reality, and not of hype.

Get it right and business news harnesses the two revolutions of our age – in information and in business – to produce greater wealth for all.

## ▶ The business revolution

Without ever understanding the role of business news, we've raced ahead in setting up the need for it. Business is now the world's prevailing philosophy. Governments of every persuasion hold that business sense makes sense. Public safety nets are being progressively dismantled. The laws that once protected us from markets – such as labour laws to guarantee job security – are being pared back because they throttle wealth creation. Companies have got ruthless about productivity. And even the public sector must make business sense now, which means market exposure and ongoing change.

We are all being challenged with riding the markets. But markets move. Industries develop. Sectors rise and fall. We've liberated our economies from all the rigidities that meant resources got locked up in low-grade and even ailing backwaters. So now all things financial are freed to change and change and change, and we can't ring-fence our own lives and livelihoods from this continuous transformation. In free currency markets, exchange rates rise and they fall. Free labour flows mean job losses and job creation.

> **This time around, ignorance is a choice not an inescapable handicap.**

That's left us all with a choice: to act with sight of the changes, or to act blind. And that choice is the only thing that makes free markets and personal responsibility for our livelihoods different from capitalism the last time around. Then, the vast majority of the population came off badly, and in many cases very badly. When Forster wrote his *Howard's End* tale of a bank clerk who lost everything by leaving a sound bank because of a rumour, to work for an ailing one that sacked him, he described a world where free markets killed ignorant people. This time around, ignorance is a choice not an inescapable handicap.

Business in the dark is gambling at hopeless odds. But once we're clear on the options, the opportunities and the risks, personal responsibility isn't just viable, it's better – and that's a promise that's drawing millions.

## Putting the newcomers in charge

Never has religion, philosophy or politics swept the world so widely or so rapidly as the conversion to business of the last two decades. The results are extraordinary by any count. Today the majority of British and American adults own businesses. They are either the owners of the businesses they run, or they've gone into big business ownership by way of the stock markets. The picture, if not quite the scale, is the same everywhere across the developed and the developing world.

Yet the unexpected face of mass capitalism is that business novices are now dictating the growth and direction of our economies. This is an outcome that has flummoxed the old-timers, not least the wizards who used to ride the stock markets to huge profits.

In 2000, Julian Robertson shut up shop on the world's second largest hedge fund, Tiger Management, saying it just wasn't possible to make money in today's 'irrational' markets. Weeks earlier and similarly bruised by the bumps in the value of the world's technology sector, billionaire financier, George Soros, had done much the same.

> ### The race to invest in the USA
>
> - Between 1980 and 1998, the proportion of households investing in mutual funds rose from 6 per cent to 44 per cent.
>
> - Between 1975 and 1998, the share of total household liquid assets held in bank savings accounts fell from 55 per cent to 23 per cent.
>
> - By 1998, Americans held $5.5 trillion in mutual funds, more than $10 trillion in stocks and just $3.7 trillion in bank savings accounts.
>
> Sources: See Note 1

But take a close look at the buying that boosted the technology sector to bubble status and a tale unfolds of the professionals being dragged along behind a whole new class of ignorant investors (see Chapter 4). Rich and poor alike, small investors with hardly any understanding of business have been pouring money into public companies' shares, affecting share prices, the behaviour of fund managers and the volatility of the stock markets.

Nowhere has this been more marked than in the USA (see box on previous page), where a quarter of US household assets are now held in the stock market.[2] Almost half of US households now own shares, including a quarter of households with incomes of less than $25,000 a year.[3] Suddenly, and as if from nowhere, ordinary people on ordinary incomes are betting their future on a market that used to be the preserve of the cognoscenti.

The same is true in the running of businesses. Small businesses are now creating most of our jobs and most of our wealth. In the USA, small business is producing more than half of the nation's total output and creating almost all of its net new jobs.[4]

This is truly a transformation. Not so long ago, small business was a byword for going nowhere. Shunned by the brightest and neglected by the powerful, it was an option for those taking their very first step up the ladder of self-improvement. However, as ex-communists have become entrepreneurs, former civil servants have entered the private sector and workers have started out on their own with just a bundle of redundancy money, small companies have become the norm across the globe.

In the USA, the majority of workers are now employed in small business. In Europe, a third of the labour force is in firms with less than ten employees and that proportion excludes all of the continent's farms.[5] For every one of these workers this is life on the business frontline. People working in a

### Europe's frontliners

Percentage of workers in non-agricultural firms of less than ten employees

|  | % |
| --- | --- |
| EU 15 | 32.8 |
| Greece | 56.5 |
| Italy | 47.8 |
| Spain | 47.5 |
| Belgium | 45.8 |
| Portugal | 38.4 |
| France | 32.8 |
| Denmark | 29.0 |
| UK | 28.9 |
| Sweden | 26.7 |
| Netherlands | 26.0 |
| Finland | 24.6 |
| Austria | 24.0 |
| Germany | 23.5 |
| Luxembourg | 22.9 |
| Ireland | 22.7 |

Source: Eurostat, March 1999

small business are not cushioned by layers of decision making. They cannot rely on another, somewhere else in a huge bureaucracy, to step in and solve the problem. Every day they must act and their actions determine their fortunes.

It's a glamorous idea. Graduates who ten years ago would have gone into banking or management consultancy would now rather run their own businesses. Even Hollywood, the most glamorous industry of all, has seen its stars diversify into entrepreneurship as the must-have status symbol. With the new millennium, the culture of the entrepreneur is gathering momentum faster than anyone could have foreseen. In four years, the number of self-employed in Britain is expected to double. In the USA, a third of Americans are thinking of starting their own businesses.

> Graduates who ten years ago would have gone into banking or management consultancy would now rather run their own businesses.

But there is one horrible hole in this fabulous success story of business for all. Most of the newcomers to business, most of the time, are operating at a massive disadvantage in terms of information and knowledge

## ▶ Illiteracy revisited

Most investors and most business owners don't understand the financial press. They are unfamiliar with basic economic concepts. They don't know how businesses work, how markets work or what mistakes cost fortunes.

We have reshaped our world in the belief that directing capital into the most efficient and strongest industries would lead to the best outcome for everyone. The dream of an enterprise culture was that each would make their own way, with a freed market drawing them to the activities that made sense.

> Most investors and most business owners don't understand the financial press.

But people who don't understand the market don't get drawn, they just go bust. Personal bankruptcies are rising rapidly – 1.3 million in the USA in 1997 alone. And businesses aren't faring much better. Between two-thirds and 90 per cent of new businesses fail (depending

## Driving blind

◆ Almost two-thirds of students and working adults don't know that inflation makes money less valuable.

◆ Only one third of adults understand that inflation helps those who have borrowed at fixed rates of interest.

◆ More than 70 per cent don't realize that GDP includes goods and services.

◆ Almost half don't know that when the government spends more than it receives there is a budget deficit.

◆ More than a third don't understand that changes in supply and demand move prices.

Source: National Council on Economic Education, *The Standards in Economics Survey*, April 1999 (www.nationalcoucil.org/poll/results.html)

on where the count is made) and the main reason is poor management.[6] 'Every survey we conduct points to the continuing failure of management to anticipate and address fundamental problems in the business for which they are responsible,' says the Society of Practitioners of Insolvency in the UK.[7]

Take a look at how little most of us know about business and that isn't surprising (see box).

In 1994, more than four-fifths of US adults who were set a basic ten-question financial literacy test in a national survey commissioned by Merrill Lynch failed.[8] In every domain of the financial world, the majority of people are moving in the dark.

There is little hope that these same financially illiterate adults will see and resolve the kinds of problems that fell businesses. The same is true when it comes to assessing other people's businesses. Small investors buy too early, sell too late and consistently lose money to the professionals (see Chapter 4). The scale of this incomprehension spells trouble ahead. With nearly half of US mutual fund investors believing diversification provides 'a guarantee that [their] portfolio won't suffer if the stock market falls', the next market correction is going to deliver a real shock to some 35 million investors.[9]

Old age is set to deliver worse than that. Over half of America's working adults have never calculated how much they need to save for their retirement.[10] And more than a third are saving nothing.[11] Even those who are saving may yet be heading for poverty on the back of wildly optimistic expectations – according to one survey, mutual fund investors anticipated returns of 22.2 per cent a year for the next decade in 1997.[12]

The bottom line is that no one can thrive acting in this kind of ignorance. In Europe, we haven't even begun to assess how equipped we all are to cope with the new order. In the USA, the SEC and other organizations are pushing hard to raise public awareness about financial issues.[13] But all the emphasis of these campaigns is on the role of schools, public interest groups, employers and government. There is barely a word about the role of the media and new media.

So, where did you learn most of what you know about business?

## News for all

You need readers. They need vision. These are the driving principles of this book. And delivering vision means thinking like a guide. It's navigation for aliens. Even business experts are aliens sometimes. In a world where we are dependent, interdependent and cross-dependent, we all need information about the places where we are not. Globalization keeps expanding the spread of events that can have a meaning for us, and the rate of change has made us desperate for clues to the future. Business readers want maps that show them where the quicksand is and where the fertile ground lies.

> Delivering vision means thinking like a guide. It's navigation for aliens.

Business news needs to come in a shape and form that people can digest and act on: with or without an opening slate of business comprehension. As an endpoint, that takes both science and art. You need a strong enough grasp of business concepts and dynamics to trace cause and effect, and the communication skills to translate that analysis into a recognizable snapshot of life.

For instance, you may realize that a company is starting to look overstretched by piecing together evidence from its three different accounts. You may see it cash-negative on the cash statement, carrying heavy interest payments on the profit and loss, and both despite a sharp tightening in working capital on the balance sheet. But pass on that analysis straight and you're talking double Dutch to most of the world's new business audience. To reach everyone, you need to go back a step to explaining why the money coming in is now less than the money going out. Then you end up with something perfectly clear – a tale of sales down or investments up and too little borrowing capacity to sustain the gap. You still use the expert numbers to support your case, but you frame them in a real-life tale of a real-life business doing business. But, more importantly, if you don't use your expertise along the way, you won't get as far. You won't spot the clues to the future, which renders the challenge of communication obsolete.

The same is true when you're writing press releases, or looking to hook readers to a corporate website. Unless you act as the expert to get to the element that matters and translate it into a tale that's recognizable to outsiders, your announcement won't get used. And it's the world's powerful need for financial literacy that dictates the element which matters (see box). Once you are working with a clear view of your readers as people in business without the maps they need, the elements that matter come down to sight of the landscape or sight of the future.

## ▶ Surveying the land

Landscape news is built upon comparison. The potential of this kind of news to deliver personal and business gain is huge. At the broadest level, it is this information that drives economic efficiency and competition. It may be the great unseen in the models of the economists, but take a look at some real examples, small and large, and the value and impact of this kind of news is clear enough.

> The proportion of professionals going to the web for information when buying new products and services more than doubled between 1998 and 1999, from 5 to 12 per cent.
>
> Source: Survey for Cahner, March 1999

In the mid-1990s, Rhône Poulenc, the French former chemicals company, cut a huge transport bill by more than a quarter, simply by collecting information on competing haulage rates.[14] Rhône Poulenc is not alone in using haulage. As a giant company it was able to fill the information gap itself by sending questionnaires to thousands of suppliers. Most businesses depend on external information services for pointers about the best and cheapest.

Without such information in the public domain, competition becomes non-existent. For example, take Kenyan interest rates. In 1996 a group of journalists spent a collective 30 hours compiling a league table of interest rates on offer to Kenyan borrowers. Until then, the banks' loan rates and conditions had never been compiled and published, which is why the spread ran from 13 per cent to 30 per cent. As long as there was no infor-mation and no comparison, there was no need to compete on price. Each

Kenyan borrower was being forced to take pot luck and the banks could charge what they liked.

Over 15 million adults in the USA claim to have researched mortgage and equity rates online.

Source: Brittain Associates, November 1998

Competition doesn't happen when customers don't know what different competitors are charging and nor does efficiency. For you, that puts a red light on any discriminatory pricing, anomalies in quality or service, or unexpected spreads. These can only exist where the flow of information is poor. And you are the flow.

Of course, we can leave it to the companies to sort it out for themselves. But think of the productive time wasted when 3000 companies around the world are simultaneously collecting data on the availability of letters of credit in south-east Asia, or the price of synthetic versus natural fibres this year. When one news service offers the relevant information kit, it reduces the international man hours expended gathering information by a four-digit multiple.

**Competition doesn't happen when customers don't know what different competitors are charging and nor does efficiency.**

This principle is already well established in personal finance reporting (see box above). Table 1.1, produced by one person and published in the *Financial Times* every Saturday, saves hundreds of individuals, seeking a home loan or mortgage, hours of phoning around to find the deal that best suits their needs (see over).

There remains huge scope in business for this kind of landscape value. Take trading in foreign markets. As soon as companies operate in another country, they become strangers abroad. Even the smallest player needs to understand foreign contract law and financial mores. They need to find foreign agents, or place staff overseas; find new transport suppliers; package and maybe advertise in different languages. Information about the state of foreign demand and tastes helps too.

Yet every multinational has this information buried in its operations. Gather it and put it out to readers on the website and it works for everyone. The multinational won't have eroded its competitive advantage, since it can decide which information to release and which to keep. But it will have achieved a well-trafficked website and a reputation as the company that

## Table 1.1: Mortgage rates comparison

**Mortgages**
Conditions, penalties and rates may vary; always check before investing.

| | Rate | Max LTV | Fee | Redemption penalty and incentive |
|---|---|---|---|---|
| **Fixed rates – without penalties** | | | | |
| Northern Rock 0845 605 0500 | 5.39% to 1.1.03 | 90% | £495 | To 1.1.03: 3/2% of sum repaid. No MIP, free ASU for 6 mths, credit cd facility |
| West Bromwich BS 0121 580 6404 | 5.49% to 31.10.02 | 95% | £295 | To 31.10.02: 3% of sum repaid. Free ASU for 1 yr, free valuation & advcs under 90%, no MIP |
| Principality BS 0800 163 817 | 5.80% to 31.12.03 | 75% | £299 | To 31:12:03: 3% of advance. |
| Derbyshire BS 0845 600 4005 | 6.20% to 31.12.03 | 95% | £195 | To 31.12.03:3/2/1% of sum repaid. £250 rebate, free valn & advcs up to 90%, no MIP. |
| **Fixed rates – with penalties** | | | | |
| Northern Rock 0845 605 0500 | 3.49% to 1.1.03 | 90% | £595 | 1st 6 yrs: 4/8/6/4/2/1% of sum repaid/benefits rec'd. Refund val'n, free ASU for 6 mths, credit cd facility & no MIP & £250 for legal fees. |
| West Bromwich BS 0121 580 6404 | 3.99% to 1.1.02 | 95% | £295 | To 31.10.05: 5/5/4/3/2% of sum repaid. Free ASU for 1 year, free valuation & advances under 90%, no MIP |
| Leeds & Holbeck BS 0800 072 5726 | 5.25% to 1.1.04 | 80% | £395 | To 1.1.06: 6 mths interest. Free MIP. |
| Scarborough BS 0870 513 3149 | 5.95% for 3 years | 95% | £395 | 1st 6 yrs: 5% of sum repaid. £1K rebate & advs up to 90%, no MIP. |
| **Capped rates** | | | | |
| Northern Rock 0845 605 0500 | 5.74% to 1.1.03 | 90% | £595 | To1.1.03:3/2% of sum repaid. Free ASU for 6 months, credit card facility & no MIP. |
| Bristol & West 0845 300 8000 | 5.79% to 1.11.02 | 95% | £299 | To 31.10.02: 5% of sum repaid. Advances up to 85%, no MIP. |
| Yorkshire BS 0845 120 0100 | 5.79% for 3 years | 75% | £495 | 1st 3 yrs: 5% of sum repaid. |
| Leeds & Holbeck BS 0800 072 5726 | 6.29% to 1.11.03 | 95% | £395 | None. |
| **First-time buyers' rates (variable unless shown)** | | | | |
| Britannia BS 0845 842 9429 | 5.34% for 2 years | 95% | £195 | Free U for 1 year & advances up to 90%, no MIP. |
| Coventry BS 0845 766 5522 | 5.50% to 31.12.02 | 95% | £195 | None Free valn & advcs up to 90%, no MIP. Remortgages, free legal fees or £200 rebate |
| Halifax 0600 203049 | 5.75% to 31.12.02 | 97% | | None. Advances up to 90%, no MIP |
| Derbyshire BS 0845 600 4005 | 5.75% for 3 yrs | 95% | £195 | None. £250 rebate, free valn & advcs up to 90% no MIP |
| **Variable discounted rates** | | | | |
| Universal Direct 08000 288383 | 5.19% for 2 years | 80% | £295 | None. No MIP. |
| Scarborough Direct 01723 355111 | 5.30% for 2 years | 95% | £150 | None. Advances up to 90%, no MIP. |
| Mercantile Direct 0500 295500 | 5.74% for 3 years | 75% | | 1st 3 yrs: 5% of sum repaid. Free U for 1 year. |
| Nationwide BS 0800 302010 | 6.09% for 3 years | 90% | | None Free valuation, free ASU for 6 months & no. MIP. |
| **Flexible Rates** | | | | |
| Scarborough Direct 01723 355111 | 6.35% for term | 95% | | None Advances up to 90%, no MIP. |
| Hinckley & Rugby BS 0800 774499 | 6.39% for term | 80% | | None Free valuation, no MIP & free ASU for 6 months. |
| Coventry BS 0845 766 5522 | 6.60% for term | 90% | | None. Free valuation & no MIP. Remtgs, free legal fees or £200 rebate. |
| Egg 0845 600 0290) | 6.69% for term | 95% | | None. Free valuation & no MIP. Remtgs, free legal fees or £200 for costs. |

MIP=Mortgage Indemnity Premium. ASU=Accident, sickness and unemployment insurance.          Source: MoneyFacts

knows about world trade. Each time the site gets recommended for its trading data or offered as a link, it's advertising for free, and readers have gained something really useful in the process.

If you want readers, you have to be giving information that delivers them real value in running their business lives, which leaves plenty of doors open.

## Predicting the future

Ignorance about the landscape is what drives most mistakes about the future. As a business writer, you can't offer an infallible crystal ball, but lots of the things that happen in business are as predictable as a car stopping because it has run out of petrol. A law change affecting imports into China hits industries and nations that trade with China. Oil prices rise when members of the Organization of Petroleum Exporting Countries (OPEC) agree in concert to limit production. The price of plastics falls when producers build too many plastic factories. Companies that invest in growing markets with little competition grow.

Placing signposts to the future requires that you spot changes today that will have consequences for your readers tomorrow. It's a matter of cause and effect. There's nothing mysterious about this. It doesn't mean writing about things that haven't happened. It means spelling out the likely consequences of the things that have happened. And this too transforms economies.

Booms and busts are caused by misplaced expectations. Robertson and Soros, the former heads of the world's largest speculative investment funds, may have thrown up their hands in despair at our irrational markets. But once small investors know more about the companies they're investing in, and about those companies' prospects, rationality may well be more evident than it was before, which means that consequences need to be part of your auto-pilot. You can hardly ever say how much or how soon, but you can be giving plenty of meaningful clues to the future – and meaningful clues as to why these events might matter to your readers. Omitting to do this is the single most common mistake of the press release. When decisions are the reason for reading, it really is critical that likely impact is part of the content.

> It's vision we sell, of here, there and beyond. Get it out of perspective and we've got it wrong

But here's the catch: overreach yourself, and overstate, and you render all that hard work worse than worthless. A misguided reader is worse off than someone who has never read your news. It's vision we sell, of here, there and beyond. Get it out of perspective and we've got it wrong. This is a fine line to tread when dealing with the future. We have to test every link as we write to check we've explained where it came from and limited ourselves to the demonstrably reasonable. Have we equipped our readers to judge what's likely more accurately than before, or have we opened the door to over-interpretation?

No matter who the audience, business news needs to be information that points us forward – so that we go with the flow rather than against it. And in the process it stabilizes the flow. Adam Smith, the founding father of economics, based the science of wealth creation on the concept that prices act as an invisible hand matching supply and demand, but in an information vacuum this often ends up as a process of last-minute clearing, causing

> **Putting a value on information**
>
> ◆ By 1995, almost one in six UK companies said it would be impossible to run their businesses for as long as six months if they lost their information.
>
> ◆ A quarter said it would take six months, or more, until their company was running normally again.
>
> ◆ Nearly a quarter said information was their most important asset.
>
> Source: *Information as an Asset: The Invisible Goldmine*, Reuters Business Information, 1995

enormous instability. Inject some unmerited optimism, a dose of fear or persistent ignorance and prices leave markets mismatched. They will eventually swing up or down to kill off or generate extra demand, but nationwide, or even globally, buyers and sellers are left glutted with stocks or cash or facing unexpected shortages.

Ending up selling at a loss is not smart business, any more than grinding to a halt because an input becomes financially out of reach. And it isn't necessary anymore. Prices are not the only way of communicating about business.

There can be no doubt that an economy well-served with information runs more smoothly. There are fewer bottlenecks, imbalances and distortions than in an economy where news is scarce (see box above).

But we really do have to get it right. We have to spot what matters, and spot what's coming. We need to sift, connect and present with clarity. This is an art as different from the old school of journalism as it is from the formal modes of business announcements. Instead of shock headlines, we must work with facts set in perspective. Instead of a warm glow about past achievements, we must concentrate on strengths and weaknesses as we piece together evidence about what the future might hold.

But it's worth the effort. Words for words' sake don't get read. But people will pay for vision that's worth more to them than the price tag. So, since we're all business minded now, let's be clear: the market is a huge one.

## ▶ Profiting from business news

Business information is the hot asset of our age. Companies steal it, the FBI monitors it, manufacturers go to court over it, moguls seek to control it, but most of all, producers are profiting from it. At a time of divided audiences and static sales for most of the rest of the media, business news is enjoying a heyday of rapid, and profitable, growth.

In the traditional media, almost every national newspaper, television channel and radio station has introduced dedicated business coverage. National and international wire services carry business news as part of their core coverage and specialist business magazines and newspapers can be counted in their thousands. This content is still evolving. New formats are emerging and styles are developing. But in this domain, at least, there are old tricks to apply and a bank of accumulated wisdom.

The same can't be said for the new media. Business news and information have become the internet's star performers. Their growth is phenomenal. In 1990, there were no corporate websites. In 2000, there will be 2.5 million.[15] Business news, advice and education sites have also proliferated. Business news has taken up pole position as the service that's succeeding in making money from the web (see box above).

## An industry in boom

◆ In the UK, the business information market grew by 74.9 per cent between 1993 and 1997.

◆ In 1998, UK sales of internet business information services rose by 104 per cent.

◆ Globally, in 1997, 23 financial information services earned a combined revenue of $15.3 bn, with four of them – Reuters, Bloomberg, Dow Jones and Bridge – together earning $4.4 bn.

◆ By mid-1997 there were 25.3 million subscribers to online services, with growth being driven by businesses signing up for news and information services.

◆ Reuters alone transmits 27,000 pages of business data every second.

Globally, CNN financial news and CBS MarketWatch were two of the first three media websites to record profits. In France, the website of business newspaper *Les Echos* is one of the country's most trafficked sites. In Germany, the circulation growth of *Börse Online*, a supposedly specialist magazine for stock market investors, has capped nearly all of the country's other publications. The pattern of success through business news is emerging everywhere. According to internet consultants, Jupiter Communications, business information services are now the model for commercial success in cyberspace.[16]

For the business news industry, need has arrived just as the infrastructure has exploded. By early 2000, there were more than 136 million people online in North America and 304 million globally.[17] This new audience likes news: better than anything else. News sites, followed by corporate sites, have become internet users' most popular ports of call.[18] In 1999, one survey found that four-fifths of internet users go online to read the web edition of newspapers – although once online they almost invariably check their e-mail first.[19]

**In the wake of mass capitalism is coming mass business news, but then the dream won't work without it.**

An earlier snapshot, looking at the types of news consumed, found 61 per cent of US users reading international and national news online, followed by 39 per cent reading business news.[20] This level of interest in business news is unprecedented, placing, as it does, business ahead of entertainment, local, technology and even sports news, in the public taste.[21]

In the wake of mass capitalism is coming mass business news, but then the dream won't work without it.

---

### 'Five People Dead, Journalists Take the Rap'

An imaginary headline, but not an imagined story.

In Ghana, in 1995, five people died in riots triggered by the introduction of value added tax. Imposed at the same rate and on the same products as the sales tax it replaced, it was not a change that would normally have led to fighting in the streets. But the journalists got it wrong.

They reported that the tax would mean much higher prices for consumers. In a country weary of painful structural adjustment policies, it was the last straw. But it wasn't true – the truth was that the journalists didn't understand the new tax and had bought a line from interest groups that stood to lose out when the tax anomalies it was targeting were ended.

Nonetheless, with the public at boiling point, the tax was abandoned, at great cost to both Ghana's economy and its people. It wasn't the first time that business news has initiated pointless suffering and even deaths. And it won't be the last.

Business news is extremely powerful: too powerful to be left in the hands of those who don't understand business.

For more information see Note 22

---

## Notes

1  Securities Industry Association, key trends in the Securities Industry During the 1990s: www.sia.org/publications/html/key_trends_3.html; Investment Company Institute, *The 1998 Mutual Fund Factbook, 63* (1998), www.ici.org/facts_figures/factbook98_toc.html; Investment Company Institute, *Trends in Mutual Fund Investing,* February 1999, www.ici.org/facts_figures/trends_0299.html; FDIC, *Quarterly Banking Profile* (December 1998).

2 Federal Reserve Board, *Flow of Funds* data March 1999.

3 Securities Industry Association estimate, given in testimony before the Senate Banking, Housing & Urban Affairs Committee, March 1999; 'Investing is not a sport', *Business Week*, 226, December 28 1998.

4 US Small Business Administration. www.sba.gov

5 Eurostat, Statistics in Focus, Industry Trade and Services no. 3, 1999. www.eubusiness.com/employ/990310es.htm

6 See Chapter 5.

7 Alan Bloom, SPI president, partner and UK head of corporate recovery at Ernst & Young, cited in press release unveiling the eight SPI survey of Company Insolvency, 10 May 1999.

8 Merrill Lynch Financial Literacy Index Analysis: a nationwide Survey of Adults, August 1994.

9 Paul Yakoboski and Jennifer Dickemper, *Increased Saving But Little Planning: Results of 1997 Retirement Confidence Survey*, Employee Benefit Research Institute Issue Brief, 1 (Nov. 1997).

10 Public Agenda/Employee Benefit Research Institute, *Promises to Keep: How Leaders and the Public Respond to Saving and Retirement*, Steve Farkas and Jean Johnson, 1994

11 *Not Your Mother's Retirement. Women and Saving in 1998*. Women's Retirement Confidence Survey for the American Savings Education Council www.asec.org/mother.htm

12 Investment Company Institute, *Investor Expectations: Mutual Fund Leaders Speak Out*, 8, 1997; www.ici.org/pdf/bro_inv-exp.pdf

13 National Council on Economic Education, *The Standards in Economics Survey*, April 1999; www.nationalcouncil.org/poll/results.html

14 'Route to big delivery savings mapped out', Jenny Luesby, 1 October 1998, *Financial Times*. www.ft.com

15 'Hard drive: cutting out the middle man', Peter Cochrane, holder of the Collier Chair for the Public Understanding of Science and Technology at the University of Bristol, *Daily Telegraph*, 11 March 1999. www.labs.bt.com/people/cochrane; www.telegraph.co.uk

16 Jupiter Communications, *Generating Revenue From Web Content*, October 1998.

17 Nua internet Surveys, www.nua.net/surveys/how_many_online/index.html

18 Media Matrix, 6 October 1998, based on survey of 30,000 internet users.

19 *Editor & Publisher*, 5 July 1999.

20 The same survey found 34.4 per cent using the internet to access sports news, 31.3 per cent for entertainment news, 25.9 per cent for local news and 20.6 per cent for technology news.

21 Jupiter Communications, December 1998, based on a survey of 2,200 internet users.

22 'VAT in Ghana: why it failed', Seth Terpker, 1996, *Tax Notes International*, 12 (23), 1801–1816.

**‘**In a world with vastly more information than it can process, journalists are the most important processors we have. The new challenge is to share this information… and to transform it into knowledge inside billions of individual brains**’**

David Shenk, Data Smog

# 2

# Getting through

## ▶ Beating a new path

Business news faces an awesome challenge of delivery. Rules of presentation are up in the air – people don't read the same way from computer screens. News value is shifting too: it's not enough to be new any more, news needs to offer the glow of enlightenment if it's going to make readers come back for more.

Also, our readers are spinning out contradictions. They want business news, but they don't understand business. They're arriving in ever greater numbers, but they're reporting information overload. They want content that's relevant to each of them individually, but they don't want to search far and wide for it. Across the board, we're grappling with the need to simultaneously span audiences and deliver relevance. It's a partnership that we're new to.

**Business news for the masses is set to move ever further from its roots in the penny sheet for investors of a century ago.**

For the time being, readers are buying anyway, because they need business information so much. But they won't tolerate the inconvenience of poor and misdirected services once better is on offer. And better is coming. Personalized – be it to the individual or to the company intranet – rich, clear, analytical, interactive, and combined with other services, business news for the masses is set to move ever further from its roots in the penny sheet for investors of a century ago. This is why, in this chapter, we begin by shaking off the values, views and ways of doing things that are holding us back. Here we look at the solutions that reconcile the apparent contradictions: solutions that we shall then build on for much of the rest of the book.

# ▶ News value

The media have only one commercial imperative – to draw and hold an audience. This is one thing the information revolution hasn't changed. But it has changed the rules of engagement. The theoretical description is commoditization, or a shift towards lower unit value. In plain terms, there's so much information on offer each piece of it is getting cheaper. When consumers can hit the web for free information, they're not interested in paying for (or often even using) a service unless it gives them something the others don't. That something extra is value added.

The news industry has always understood value added: circulation wars go back to the media industry's earliest days. But traditionally supremacy came down to just three selling points:

◆ being first

◆ exposing the most

◆ offering the greatest accuracy.

This left the news value dilemma centred around a single decision: did a news service go after scoops or sell itself as a service of record.

News value is not nearly so simple today. For a start, the old beacons have all but disappeared. Technology has made rapid news delivery almost universal. There are still news services that thrive on the back of instant, as-it-happens coverage. But short of a James Bond scenario, where the media mogul creates the news in order to ensure that his empire is indeed first with the facts, there is no way of getting there faster. For most news services, timeliness is something they just must deliver, as a matter of course. It doesn't win them readers, it's simply a prerequisite.

Similarly, the value of accuracy has been greatly diminished by the web. Consumers certainly demand accuracy from their news services, but when they can go straight to the source material themselves, accuracy in the relaying is hardly a selling point in it's own right.

Even the scoop is not the bull's-eye it once was. It may bring kudos in professional circles, but it makes little odds to readers that you were first when your exposé has become a run-of-the-mill story on hundreds of other news services – within hours.

In short, in an era when the competition for audiences is more intense than it has ever been, news services are being forced to rethink what makes news outstanding. First, accurate and farthest still make up the foundations of a strong news service, but they are not the ingredients that pull audiences.

In fact, the new icon is wisdom. News services that do well are those that provide the most wisdom for the least reader effort. This is the new mark of quality. But it requires a profound shift in mindset. Like manufacturers, who over the last 20 years have torn themselves away from the old way of making first and selling second, we are having to learn to make what sells. It's a transition that's harder than we think, because it means breaking with a past of newsroom machismo. We like the cut and chase of doing what we can with what turns up on any one news shift. It's an adrenalin ride we're used to. But it's an effort that's misdirected. Readers judge what we write by what it gives them. And on that basis first isn't best. The most enlightening is the best.

> **News services that do well are those that provide the most wisdom for the least reader effort.**

This is a reality that puts the reader centre stage. We can be fast, accurate and original without the slightest understanding of our audience. But we can't, and won't, deliver enlightenment until we understand our readers' agenda. Only then does it matter who delivers the enlightenment fastest.

## ▶ News agenda

But enlightenment about what? Knowledge is only as valuable as we feel it is. If you want to hit the button with readers, you need to understand what set them hunting for knowledge in the first place.

In fact all news has an emotional agenda. There have to be reasons why any one story appeals. It may titillate, or reassure. It may reinforce a sense of community, or unite readers against a common enemy. But it always connects with something in our readers' emotional make-up. This is the art of the communicator – to make information compelling. Business news doesn't need drama to do this, or shock headlines. We are operating in a world of uncertainty that's frightening and destabilizing. What we do is put people back into the driving seat. Our emotional pay-off is invincibility. Read business news, stay on top of what's happening in the world and you can rule the waves. This is our message.

Once you grasp that, it dictates a new way of working. You stop cramming in every last detail and loose thread. You stop creating an ever ticking ticker tape. You calm right down and deliver with authority and pace. You concentrate upon cause and effect, comparison and perspective, because it is these that deliver understanding. And understanding is the key.

> Read business news, stay on top of what's happening in the world and you can rule the waves. This is our message.

Once a reader understands the cause of a problem, it becomes predictable and even scalable. That's much less frightening than incomprehension. Causes also open the door to solutions, or at least a bypassing of the problem. By reporting how others have resolved this one, you offer more still. Without learning from others we are forced to invent everything ourselves, which is inevitably slower than a pooling of bright ideas.

But, perhaps most importantly of all, understand the emotional hook and it becomes obvious that stories that leave critical questions hanging only serve to reinforce a reader's sense that events are moving faster than they can keep pace with. With an incomplete story you're saying it can't be known or that you're not a competent source.

This is why so many managers express exasperation (as we shall see in the next chapter) at the inadequacy and irrelevance of the news they receive. They're being flooded with information by providers who don't realize that unanswered questions are a kick in the teeth.

'This is all you need to know' is the most fetching message of them all. *The Economist* magazine knows this, but others in the business media have lost their way on this one. Pumping up the content, the volume, the spread, the criteria, and at the same time missing identifiably important elements, doesn't deliver reassurance. It just communicates confusion and becomes alarming in its own right. Because we work with fear, we have to move with confidence. And that means certainty about which stories, and what information, matters most.

# Must-have analysis

Analysis is not an optional extra in business news. Our mission is to inspire confidence, not just in our reporting, but in the reader's decision making, which means setting things in perspective.

When we've scaled an event and made clear who might be affected, how, and why, we've answered the questions. All our readers ever really want to know is who's copping this change, for better or for worse: or even who's winning and who's losing on the basis of the current status quo. This is the information that takes the fear out of change or opens the door to gains.

**Stories about flesh-eating bugs may frighten, but they won't bring our health service to its knees.**

Report winners and losers without this analysis and we're into a whole other ball game. It's not a new one. This is old territory for the general media. From AIDS to mad cow disease, child abductions to the mugging of pensioners, the shock of the innocent loser has long been a big seller for newspapers. It's frightening stuff. But it's not dangerous in the same way as shocks about business.

Stories about flesh-eating bugs may frighten, but they won't bring our health service to its knees. The same dramatic licence applied to house prices, recession, a company's performance, a market's mood or a bank's credibility will be self-fulfilling. Say there are losers and people will pull out, which means there will be losers. People act on business news, because gains reported out of perspective produce a similarly horrible outcome – as can be seen with the get-rich-quick journalism that has emerged as the core of the first wave of populist business news.

This type of news is about easy and instant wealth for all – the business and stock market equivalents of winning the lottery. The trouble is, of course, it's a chimera and the stakes are so much higher than in most other types of fantasy fortune-hunting. The loss of a £1 lottery stake is unlikely to count as a personal tragedy, but readers back the recommendations of these new news services with their life savings.

© Roger Beale

> **66** Journalism ... is an opportunity to give information that can change or even save people's lives. **99** [1]

Which is the attraction for most of the journalists who go into it. But business journalists shift people's expectations, confidence and spending decisions – en masse. And that can wreak havoc.

For more information see Footnote 1.

While this kind of hype makes things soar, they don't stay airborne. When reality starts to make itself felt, the crash wrecks lives, which is a lot of pain to cause for no good reason. Journalists who peddle false hopes are not like entertainers who lift our hearts for a few hours by portraying heaven. From the Asian bubble to the internet bubble, over-investment depends on a loss of perspective. (See box.)

This is something that general news has never had to grapple with. No one expects a murder report to tell us how many times the victim previously walked safely down that road. General news can scope its subject and deliver from a single angle. But the value of our words to readers rests on our ability to convey an accurate picture – not all at once, not all in the same story, but piece by piece and overall. Only when we say: this is how it is, this is what it means and these are the options, do we inspire confidence and trigger the emotional pay-off.

## Delivering quality

So, why should I care about the Guatemalan economy these days? You tell me. Work incredibly hard at collecting your information and balancing it all and drawing the key themes and key implications, and then give me a beautiful simple map that makes it plain inside a single page for less than ten minutes' reading.

**Readers want insight that you've sweated for, not newsflashes that you've dashed for.**

This is what readers mean by high quality content, that is, the stuff they rate and return for (see box). Breathless updates about meaningless trivia are fooling no one.

Readers want insight that you've sweated for, not newsflashes that you've dashed for. The newsflash is only valuable as a signpost to more, or as a niche service for the pre-informed – when an audience knows everything but the latest twist, they might well regard the last snippet as valuable on its own. For the rest it's just more meaningless data.

Be careful, too, if you're going for speed rather than extra labour on the grounds of feasibility. Putting out newsflashes because newsflashes are what's easy to deliver, is not at all the same thing as doing it because that's what serves the reader best.

The truth is that news a fact at a time is exactly what is creating information

### Why they return

US users on their favourite websites

|  | % |
| --- | --- |
| High quality content | 75 |
| Ease of use | 66 |
| Quick download | 58 |
| Frequent updates | 54 |
| Coupons and incentives | 14 |
| Favourite brands | 13 |
| Cutting edge technology | 12 |
| Games | 12 |
| Purchasing capabilities | 11 |
| Customizable content | 10 |
| Chat | 10 |

Source: See Note 3

overload. 'We're scrambling here but here [pant] is the last thing that we heard' may make us feel good, but it leaves readers racing to keep up – as if they weren't racing enough already. It is, in short, a waste of our readers' time, as more than 60 per cent of business executives (and rising) have now concluded.[2] They are only too clear that dilution is the enemy. Instead of restoring control, huge amounts of low-grade and unhelpful information just add a new burden as they are sifted through in search of a nugget.

Measured, discerning, thoughtful, complete – this is information that feels good, and gets used.

## ▶ News formats

Time is short. Things are moving fast. Value is measured in time expended as well as knowledge gained, which means that for the consumer finding news has to be easy, as well as rewarding.

The average internet user spends less than ten minutes a session accessing news, and even readers of the traditional media surf. Just try giving yourself a fixed ten minutes in each of two, three or four different news sites and you're going to find that your hurry creates some demanding imperatives:

1  Simplicity of design is a huge bonus – hit one of those higgledy-piggledy, jam everything in home pages and you'll have eaten up your ten minutes just trying to make sense of it all.

2  Signposting is absolutely critical – without it the most wonderful content is just lost.

3  The debate over whether it is better to deliver news as soundbite menus or indepth analysis is entirely false. To really get something from a site, you need both: the snippet summaries that act as signposts and the internal completeness that makes a piece satisfying once you've reached it.

Indeed, while you're performing this exercise, have a think about the news stories that you do end up reading. How do they leave you feeling? If they don't draw a moment of satisfaction, be sure: they were a waste. They won't have left anything with you that you'll ever use again. It's also worth noticing which reads are the most rewarding. There's an idea we've been entertaining for a while that we just can't pack as much information into news delivered electronically. Maybe it's rooted in the fact that we all read 20 per cent slower onscreen. But the slowness of scrolling, the flicker rate and all the other elements of electronic communication that make it harder than reading from paper mean one thing only: readers won't tolerate dilution. Copy that rambles is out. News that wanders is off. Depth is not just possible, it's the only way of keeping people. When each new line adds something really germane, or answers the question raised by the previous piece of information, readers are far less likely to sign out before the end. And when they do go, they'll leave with something worth having.

> **Depth is not just possible, it's the only way of keeping people.**

So you need to exploit every type of format to get the easiest access to the most depth. Readers like places where they can scoop up quick hits. So design them. You also need to rethink your ideas about space. If you lock yourself into four fab facts a day, it won't be long until there are only two fab facts that day and two sadly mediocre ones. Be willing to leave two blanks. Really. It's better.

Mediocre is just not good enough, as most of us have long since observed when chasing a trail of links that don't link. There are few things more frustrating than following someone's link to another source of information, only to find that this recommended source is not just low grade, but completely irrelevant. If a reader is left wondering why on earth a link was given, it shouldn't have been. It's diluting satisfaction, not enhancing it. (See box.)

Similarly, pictures and graphics need to communicate more in less time than words. Off-line that depends on the image. Online it rests on the download time. It's not worth having an illustration – not a logo, not a banner, not anything – if it means readers have disappeared before the piece is on the screen.

### Getting personal

Business news services have evolved as a jumble of information because they've been seeking to satisfy thousands of disparate information needs simultaneously.

Technology is opening the door to consumer-controlled filters, which will prolong the life of the specialist-news-for-all service. It won't matter that everything is coming down a single line if readers can dispense with the irrelevant before it arrives.

But filters cannot create the quality in the first place.

> The more control we facilitate, the more valuable we are.

At every turn, format must be about satisfaction. Readers want their questions answered, so we need to be exploring the limits of the frequently asked questions format, taking it as far as we can to a personalized information service. And we need to offer bolt-on information, like availability services, or tailored directories relating to specific topics. The more control we facilitate, the more valuable we are.

Even the 90-second financial headline summary – which appears to fly in the face of value based on knowledge gained – offers greater control. Barebones stuff, it's enough to trigger a search for more information if there really is something important happening, but otherwise it reassures the reader or listener that they are missing nothing. And that's a result on the invincibility count.

Format is one of our greatest aids in making information easy to digest. Undigested it isn't knowledge. So just imagine the format that would work for you: and you have a blueprint.

## ▶ Our markets

Audiences matter, and some are easier to satisfy than others, which is why the industry has developed so unevenly. In some areas business news is becoming overcrowded. In others, it's a relic: either a bung-everything-through service left over from the days when information was a scarce resource, or a literary rendition of a statistical digest, designed when people had time – and the willingness – to plough through the deadly dull.

> Audiences matter and some are easier to satisfy than others, which is why the industry has developed so unevenly.

The most advanced area, by far, is news for investors in public companies. Business news has more history in this than in other areas. This is also an audience that from Britain to Romania has been boosted widely by windfall share bonuses and employee share-ownership schemes. As a result, national newspapers now serve up a steady fare of company news and economic commentary for shareholders. Investors are also well served by the new media, with the stock market reporting that was once dominated by the wires now the fare of countless dot.coms.

It is certain that the overcrowding in this one sector will give way to a shakedown in the near future. Geography will preserve some services: German investors most want to read about German companies. But online suppliers, with their global reach, will steadily erode this barrier. Ultimately, success in this market depends on doing what a lot of people are doing better. That means services that run the gamut from news alert to research facility, and all of it meaningful to the newcomer. It means comparisons between strong and weak performers, and it means a great deal of information about what the big investors – the investment funds – are doing. In short, it's everything that converts the small investor of today into the rational investor of tomorrow.

**The other area of galloping growth is personal finance.**

The other area of galloping growth is personal finance, which has exploded on the back of a single characteristic. Most aspects of personal finance are relevant to nearly all of us. Millions take out a mortgage. We nearly all pay taxes. Most of us run credit cards. Of all business news, personal finance enjoys the largest potential audience, with the greatest overlap in interests. Structuring coverage to this audience is simplicity itself compared with the diverse demands of businesses. But personal finance still faces the challenge of educating as it informs. It has gone further with this than other types of business news. But coverage can still be horribly arcane. In future, this news will be put together with a good deal more wit and verve. It will also – like investor news – evolve steadily into a one-stop shop, combining news with buying and selling services.

However, large as the equity investment and personal finance audiences are, these two sectors will ultimately represent just a fraction of the business information market. Over the next few decades it will be news to entrepreneurs and to businesses that will see, and cause, a revolution. The slow take-off in this news is a consequence of the greater need for innovation, not the lack of demand. As we find ways to customize content for managers and present new business in a way that opens the door to all, these sectors will take over as the core of business news.

Quite simply, in our personal lives and as investors, our business decisions are occasional, albeit important. Owners and managers, however, are on a treadmill of decision making. Their need for information ranges across time, space and subject, but it is constant. Managers don't get to a point where they've taken out their mortgage, and they're on a five-year breather until they start saving for school fees. Their whole job, 40 or more hours a week is about taking decisions, informed or not.

So, here we are, with a diverse and needy public pushing the business news industry faster than many information providers can move. Millions of corporate websites are seeking a direction, intranets are burgeoning, but not necessarily assisting, and news services are jostling for position. In a world glutted with information, only the truly useful will flourish. As an industry, it's an exciting place to be. It has not all been done before. There will be new and better ways. And what they will do is enable us to deliver signals through all that noise.

> **In a world glutted with information, only the truly useful will flourish.**

## Notes

1    Quote from a 1999 survey of 552 journalists conducted by the Pew Research Centre.

2    *Glued to the Screen: An Investigation into the Effects of Information Addiction Worldwide*, Reuters Studies, December 1997, www.reuters.com/rrb/research/addict.htm

3    *Strong Content Means a Loyal Audience*, Forrester Research, 27 January 1997. Findings based on a survey of 8,600 US households.

'More information has been
produced in the last 30 years than in the
previous 5000. A weekday edition of the
New York Times has more information in it
than the average 17th century man or woman
would have come across in an entire lifetime.
About 1000 books are published
internationally every day, and the total
of all printed knowledge doubles
every five years'

Dr David Lewis

# 3

# Meeting the managers

## ▶ A poisoned chalice

For managers, who consume more information than any of the rest of us, the noise is deafening. They collect so much information that academics are starting to call them addicts. Yet ask them how much they get from it, and the answers are gloomy. Most say the information they get isn't worth the effort. They say the things they want the most are the hardest to find. More than half report a high when they actually do manage to track something down. Addiction this may be, but it's also a mighty mismatch between what's on offer and what managers want.

> For managers, who consume more information than any of the rest of us, the noise is deafening.

There's really no excuse for this in an era supposedly driven by knowledge. Either managers can be informed, and we are the ones who are going to do it. Or they can't, in which case let's pack up the information age and go home. That would certainly be better than getting it wrong. We're going to look aplenty in this chapter at what we need to do to provide indispensable information to managers. But before we do, in just this one place, we're going to look at the costs of ill-judged news. This is not an exercise in $ or Euros. It's evidence we need to hear. Information, it turns out, can be a poisoned chalice. If we allow it to be.

## ▶ Paying for inundation

Managers – a category that accounts for more than 10 per cent of the world's labour force – should really be our most avid customers. Worldwide, and at every level of seniority, they depend on information. Of 1,000 managers surveyed by Reuters in 1996, only 30 said they made decisions on gut instinct. Nearly 700 said they needed 'a lot of information' to do their jobs and 300 said they needed 'an enormous amount'.[1]

### Waste ... and more waste

◆ Executives spend an average of 60 per cent of their working time reading.

◆ Around 70 per cent of the information companies buy is never used.

◆ Less than half of managers use information to make decisions. The majority collect it 'to justify' choices.

Source: See Note 2

Yet the very scale of their need is driving their mounting frustration at what we're offering.

Today's business managers are living life in a race where every step can bring a stumble. In deciding which potential market to chase, which supplier to buy from, or which information source to search, they can create profits, or gobble them up. This is a lot of responsibility to live with. Yet managers are progressively cramming more decisions into the same amount of time, which means less time for research. They are left craving information that they are not getting and, thanks to us, cannot get.

**Today's business managers are living life in a race where every step can bring a stumble.**

So acute is their lack of information that knowledge has become a political weapon. 'It's gotten to a stage where you cannot come to a decision without worrying that someone might have more information than you and could make your decision look wrong', said one telecommunications manager based in Singapore.[3] As a result, managers are buying more information than they need to do their job and processing more than is valuable to their employers – just because they are scared of missing the vital. However the outcome is exactly that (see box above).

Too much information drags us down. Managers, financial analysts and information workers inundated with data, make more mistakes, misunderstand others, and snap at co-workers and customers, according to research by Dr David Lewis, author of one of the Reuters Studies on Information Overload.[4] They also draw flawed conclusions and make foolish decisions that cost companies money.

Information is even costing managers their personal lives: as hours get longer, data-processing spills into the home, and workplace stress rises.

> **The verdict on information**
>
> ◆ 47 per cent of managers say **people are being distracted from their job responsibilities**.
>
> ◆ 43 per cent say **important decisions are being delayed**.
>
> ◆ 42 per cent say **individual decision making is suffering**.
>
> ◆ 41 per cent say **individuals aren't seeing the full picture**.
>
> ◆ 37 per cent say **vital details are being missed**.
>
> Source: Reuters, *Dying for Information*

Having switched on the information tap, managers are proving unable to deal with the flow. Which is not surprising. According to psychologists, the human brain just isn't built to process such a vast volume of input. 'Our brains aren't wired to "multi-task" the way computers are. We're taxing our human abilities to the limit,' says one.[5] (See box.)

## The relief of the filter

Time-strained managers want information that gives maximum firepower for minimum effort. In this they are not alone. We all want to get things that are new, profound and pertinent from what we read, and not just with business news. In the UK, the nation's fastest growing news magazine, *The Week*, has no correspondents and no specialists. Instead, its 20 editorial staff act as strategic filters, condensing the best from everywhere else. The news, editorials, comments, letters and even the funnies, are summarized, with briefings on complex running stories, and a

> **Time-strained managers want information that gives maximum firepower for minimum effort.**

© Roger Beale

touch of panache. No more wading through 100 pages of broad-sheet newsprint for 10 good stories. *The Week* offers 40 A4 pages packed with gems: and consumers love it.

### Noise

US office staff get an average of 201 messages a day – at a minute a message that's more than three hours of processing every day.

They get interrupted by calls and messages needing an immediate answer every 10 minutes.

The web just grew by 76 pages while you read this sentence.

Source: See Note 6.

Its real beauty is that it delivers depth as well as breadth. The biggest running stories are subdivided into facts, comments and outlook. The aim is not just to keep readers abreast of the news, but also of the news agenda, by highlighting the unresolved, the upcoming and the developments that may follow. In sum, *The Week* makes it very easy, and very quick, to be informed. Which is why it is driving up the sales rankings with growth of almost 50 per cent a year.

Compare that with the rest of the British media and you will begin to see the difference that quality makes to sales. Where other suppliers have sought to push up revenue by producing extra pages, supplements and parallel channels, *The Week* has captured the consumer by offering the most enlightenment for the least effort. In this, it represents the future of business information.

The economist Steffan Linder, a quarter of a century ahead of his time, predicted the problem of data overload, as just one element in an imminent 'time famine'. He also foresaw the solution that is now emerging. Once time is at a premium, managers turn to paid professionals for significant information, and dump the rest.

## ▶ Gearing to strategic relevance

If what we are selling is our time and capacity to sift out what matters, we need to understand what managers are looking and listening for. In fact, above all else, they want to know who or what they're up against (see box overleaf).

> **❝ Only unintelligent buyers acquire complete information ❞**
>
> Steffan Linder, *The Harried Leisure Class*, Columbia University Press, 1970

They want to know what their **competitors** are doing, what decisions they are taking, what their plans are, what strategies they are following, and what their strengths and weaknesses are.' This same information is what investors seek (see Chapter 4), which puts company news at the top of the value chart whatever the information service – it is something almost all business readers want.

The other core coverage for managers is information about **markets**, which means what people are buying and what they want to buy, as well as the practical realities of serving consumers. These two areas, and **technology** news – covering both products and processes – represent the biggest information gaps for managers (see above). There's a reason for this.

In each of these three areas **information can deliver competitive advantage**: and it is this that lies at the heart of strategic relevance. The reason journalists find it hard to get this information and make it public, is because every business wants it only for itself. Which is not to say that

## The information managers want and how hard it is to find

|  | Value | Ease of finding | Frequency of use |
| --- | --- | --- | --- |
| Competitors | Very important | Very difficult | Very frequently |
| Markets | Very important | Quite difficult | Very frequently |
| Technology | Quite important | Difficult | Quite frequently |
| Resources | Quite important | Quite easy | Quite frequently |
| Regulation | Opinion divided | Opinion divided | Opinion divided |
| Global issues | Not important | Easy | Seldom |

From a survey of managers in the Portuguese chemicals industry
Source: Zita Correia and T.D. Wilson, *Scanning the Business Environment for Information: a Grounded Theory Approach*

> **❝ Information is only as valuable as it is useful ❞**
>
> David Shenk, Data Smog, Abacus, 1997

it becomes worthless if everyone has it. It's like any leap forward. Once a farmer has a tractor, he will produce more and earn more than his neighbour with a horse and plough. When everyone has a tractor, his advantage will have been eroded – but the world will have more.

Better information about the factors that confer competitive advantage enhances efficiency and hastens progress (see box opposite). Patents and copyright exist for companies who have devised something extraordinary. Our society deems that these businesses have the moral right to profit from their brilliance. But the whole point of the information age is that it is blowing away competitive advantage based on one company having information that others don't.

**The whole point of the information age is that it is blowing away competitive advantage based on one company having information that others don't.**

The farmer with the tractor will earn less once everyone else has one, but what was the particular reason why he should be the only farmer to benefit? His astuteness and financial organization in buying a tractor early gave him a head start. He has profited more than most will by being ahead of the leap. Fine. Now let's tell everyone how much better it is.

So, information that is hard to get is that way because everyone wants to have it, and no one wants to give it. Conversely, the information managers find easy to obtain (and value little) is data that other people or organizations *want* them to notice. **Resources** – that is, information about the financial, labour and raw material markets that serve businesses – is about the things that companies *buy*. Of course it's easy to get. In PR, they call much of this reporting free advertising. Similarly with **regulatory** news, governments may not be very good at informing us all about the rules, but they do want us to know.

Finally, there is the information about the social, cultural, demographic, economic and political trends that go to make up **global issues**. Managers value this little, and journalists love to write about it. It may be *because* journalists favour it so much that managers dismiss its importance – on the basis that they are so well served they rarely, if ever, have to go hunting for this information.

But managers' disregard for reporting on aggregate trends also speaks to the peculiarly abstract way in which much of this news is reported. Managers are operating in real and very specific circumstances. Big picture news is only meaningful when it comes across as real and relevant, which means relating it to life as we live it.

> ## Playing radar screen
>
> Competitive advantage doesn't just lie with learning about what's new and changing. Competent management is crucial.
>
> In the UK, most company failures are caused by poor management. In 1998 alone, management failings caused 58 per cent of the country's insolvencies directly, and contributed to another 22 per cent – they also caused the loss of more than 100,000 jobs.[8]
>
> Managers are frequently unaware of issues that need addressing. Which is why you must explain the significance of your stories: who is going to be affected and how. Only then will you catch the eyes of those who have not already made the connection.
>
> You also need to be looking for areas where managers are consistently making mistakes or underperforming.
>
> Above all things, you need to become adept at spotting the first signs of things coming their way.

## Making it stick

The lives of human beings are what make stories stick. A manager's main data store, despite all our efforts to build electronic add-ons, remains his memory. And readers remember things better when they are built around personal drama – as in real lives. Mathematical equations make the eyes glaze.

**Remembering business news matters.** Information that lodges will be used to inform decisions months, or even years, later. It will also get drawn on across a range of activities –peripheral to some, central to others, and it will be valued all the more highly for being available for everything.

> Knowledge implies enlightenment. When we tell a story about people, managers end up understanding the subject differently.

This is critical to services that are built as a continuous flow. We can build content that is useful, but we will never be able to deliver it all at precisely the right time. If readers recognize it as useful, they may file it. Or they may remember it later, and go looking for it. Neither is efficient – according to one study managers spend 150 hours a year on average trying to find information they know they have somewhere.[9]

This waste is part of what has spawned the fuss within management science over the difference between information and knowledge. Information is just data. We can waste a lot of time searching for it and piecing it together to make sense. Knowledge implies enlightenment. When we tell a story about people, managers end up understanding the subject differently. They can apply this with or without finding the article again.

Indeed, you must have read stories like this. I remember one about the Bulgarian rose industry, a news analysis in the *FT* some time in the mid-1990s. It left me understanding things about roses, the perfume industry, eastern European agriculture and even the implications of the end of communism, which have stayed with me since. Strangely, when something sticks like that it gets used, even when it seems to be outside our remit (the world is a place of global and cross-related industries). Enlightenment also leaves you appreciating the source – the stirrings of customer loyalty you might say – and that matters too.

Information that managers hunt for once a particular problem has been identified may put a particular news service into a manager's sights. But news services want regular viewers (or the advertisers won't pay). It is not enough to rely on drawing regular traffic to a service's archives with a solid diet of useful data: managers don't have enough time for research and their success in searching things out, anyway, depends on how much they know to start with.

> Delivering of enlightenment, rather than shovelling of data, requires that you make your copy sing. No song, no knowledge.

Continuous services need to build an ever-increasing bank of knowledge to equip managers to do the most with the least. This delivering of enlightenment, rather than shovelling of data, requires that you make your copy sing. No song, no knowledge.

## ... and lighting the path forward

Journalists do so like spotting problems. Writing about solutions is not as enticing (and quite likely to invoke the scorn of news editors hooked on mess-ups and crises). But it's solutions that managers are after. Most of the time, they are playing Mr FixIt, which means discovering new and better ways of doing things. They find premises, implement new investments, run marketing campaigns They buy equipment, arrange finance, billing and transport. They oversee research, communications and product design.

> 66 Navigation ... is likely to be the fulcrum around which competitive advantage hinges 99
>
> Philip Evans and Thomas S. Wurster, *Blown to Bits: How The New Economics of Information Transforms Strategy*, Harvard Business School Press, 2000

Finding new and better ways of doing things depends on outsiders and information about outsiders. Without this information, every step forward involves reinventing the wheel, which is why the management gurus are calling our industry 'navigation'. If the producers of business information aren't offering 3-D relief maps with all the important features marked, who will?

It is up to us to produce information that will help managers find their way around. Grasp this, and we will have cracked the code on their information hunger. So here's how we do it:

1 Identify the audience for every story you write.

2 Be clear about the decision you're helping with.

3 Become the decision-maker.

4 Always look to the future.

5 Make it a story about human beings.

6 Make it findable.

7 Don't send stories to people who won't want them.

## Identify the audience for every story you write

No news is worth reporting if no one is going to be affected. There have to be people interested in starting businesses in Hong Kong to merit a piece on the subject. There must be manufacturers who depend on soda ash to make it worth reporting the likelihood of a price rise. And there must be managers organizing the delivery of a surge of goods bought online to justify a piece on couriers versus mail.

> It is up to us to produce information that will help managers find their way around.

Once you've identified the audience, tell the rest of us how big it is, because we all want to understand the significance of this story. Is this an issue for 100 bike manufacturers or eight pharmaceutical companies (or 200,000 hospital patients)? When delivering news of a company's change in strategy, tell us how many competitors are going to feel the ripples. Give us a technology story – and tell us how many producers are using the old model (that is, how many potential buyers there are). Focus on a market and scale the industry that supplies it. The audience *is* the significance.

## Be clear about the decision you're helping with

It is this that drives the content. Like any high school essay, business news needs to address a question, or related questions. Only then will you put together the piece that satisfies. Understanding the decision puts you in a position where you are asking the same questions as your audience. Suppose you're writing a story about a bank, you might be addressing a wide audience of shareholders, managers and consumers, but they are all facing the same decision: do I want to have dealings with this bank? With that in mind you head for the quality of its service (is it competitive?); soundness of its strategy (is it going to get itself into – or out of – trouble?); it's record (is the management competent?); and any examples of its morality (will it screw me?). By getting the decision clearly in your sights, the content becomes self-evident.

## Become the decision-maker

You will only start asking **real** questions, when you have become the one facing the decision. Take a logistics manager assessing couriers as an option. He'd love to know how (and whether) others get a discount, and so will you, once you've started getting into readers' heads. Managers want to know how much things cost (hard to get), and smart ways of making savings. So think like it's *your* budget at stake.

## Always look to the future

A glorious, human being filled, comprehensive feature on the mechanics of company registration in China is worth nothing if you don't mention that pressure is building for a moratorium on new entrants. The story a manager is reading today can only ever be applied in the future. You need to cover the present and the past only insofar as they throw light on the imminent. In the business news timeline, the future is *always* the only time that matters.

## Make it a story about human beings

Once you've got the picture, there's no call for abstract art. Make it real, and make it live. Images, data and quotes make meaningful information easy to digest.

## Make it findable

No matter how relevant and how vivid a piece, if a reader can't locate it, your time has been wasted. A website, database or news service without a search engine fails the first test of ease of use, by preventing managers from jumping straight to the subject they seek. The same is true with off-line information that is marketed without an index. This is just a good way of burying the relevant.

Every business reader is a specialist, homing in on subject-specific headlines, before dipping into matters of more general interest. Don't leave them watching the traffic – give them a signpost.

## Don't send stories to people who won't want them

One of the greatest challenges in getting information through to managers lies in stopping the irrelevant. News has to be shaken down into separate feeds for different interest groups, even where it all comes through the same channel.

Indeed, this is the beauty of the intranet. Far from being an opportunity to give more information to managers, it is a chance in a million to make sure they get less. Take information centrally, slice it by subject, and you have

### Making it useful

1  There must be an audience whose decisions will be affected.

2  The information should be focused around the decision in question.

3  It should be comprehensive but tightly presented.

4  It must look ahead.

### ...and making it useable

5  It needs to reflect life in order to be memorable.

6  It must be locatable by index, or preferably a keyword search.

7  It should not be sent to audiences who are unaffected.

consigned to one job the filtration that is currently being repeated, and repeated, and repeated, by different managers throughout an organization. And then managers have the time to get more!

## ▶ Why we have to do it

Do you ever play logic chains – when you're driving, in the bath, wherever – like this: if 70 per cent of managers use a great deal of information in their jobs, and more than 10 per cent of the world's labour force are managers, that's more than 7 per cent of the labour force using a great deal of the kind of information we've been talking about. That's a *lot* of information, which means you can bet your life that there are a large number of people earning a living building information for managers (P.S. if you don't, you should – logic chains drive news).

The industry that supplies managers with information is about to get a whole lot more competitive – and a lot of people are going to be affected as buyers and sellers; which makes it pretty big news.

As things stand, news suppliers are selling information that managers are dissatisfied with, but buy anyway. All that's needed to upset this status quo is a new class of information providers, really hungry for audiences. As they move to supply better, more satisfying services, the old guard are going to find their jobs disappearing as their sales do.

So who are these new suppliers? The key is electronic commerce. Electronic trading between businesses is being heralded as the next marketing revolution. Some researchers are forecasting electronic sales between businesses – that is, business to business, or B2B – of more than $4 trillion by 2003.[10]

B2B commerce that uses electronic networks and the internet to automate ordering, invoicing and delivery procedures to **pre-selected** customers is growing rapidly. But these estimates are based on an escalation in **open-door** selling to managers: that is, where a small business in Scotland, a manager in a middle-sized German company, a buyer in a Korean national industry and anyone else can sign on, order and pay. At the moment, this kind of trade is growing only slowly. In time, it is inevitable that it will start to gallop. It offers the potential of being quicker and cheaper. Once suppliers have got it organized so that it pays, managers will have to switch over, or justify the cost of not doing so.

> **Electronic trading between businesses is being heralded as the next marketing revolution.**

In the meantime, managers aren't buying, but **they are using the internet to get business news and information**. This means that news services are emerging as the main platform for businesses trying to reach their customers electronically. In March 2000, AdRelevance reported a surge in B2B advertising channeled primarily through computer/technology, business/finance and general news sites.

But this is about more than a take-off in advertising: information services are poised to become the forum for the e-commerce. What B2B advertisers and sellers will be chasing are services with a captured managerial audience – hence the new information suppliers, or a new face for the old suppliers.

Navigators aren't just going to spring into being because managers want them – navigators will emerge because there is an opportunity to make profits selling managers the information they want.

## Notes

1 *Dying for Information? An Investigation Into The Effects Of Information Overload In The UK And Worldwide*, Reuters Business Information, 1996, p. 17.

2 Executive Reading Time: www.evelynwood.com.au; Library waste: Leonard M. Fuld and Kent Potter, 1999, *CIO Enterprise Magazine*, 15 June; Information for decision-making versus justification: *ibid* 1, p. 20, Q.5.

3 *Ibid* 1, p. 23.

4 *Ibid* 1, pp. 2–3.

5 Larry Rosen, psychology professor at California State University, cited in Bridget Murray, 1998, 'Data smog: newest culprit in brain drain', *American Psychological Association Monitor*, 29 (3). www.apa.org/monitor/mar98/smog.html

6 Messages and Interruptions: 'Pitney Bowes "Workplace Communication in the 21st Century"; Web Growth', NEC Research Institute, 1999.

7 S. Goshal, 'Environmental scanning: an individual and organizational analysis', cited in Z. Correia, *Scanning the Business Environment: A Grounded Theory Approach*, T.D. Centre for Technical Information for Industry, National Institute for Engineering, Lisbon. *Information Research*, 2(4) (www.shef.ac.uk/~is/publications/infres/paper21.html)

8 *Eighth Survey of Company Insolvency in the UK*, Society of Practitioners of Insolvency, May 1999.

9 Hemphill & Associates, Raleigh, New Carolina, 1998.

10 Gartner Group research, January 2000.

'Markets need a fresh
supply of losers just as
builders of the ancient
pyramids of Egypt needed
a fresh supply of slaves'

Dr Alexander Elder,
Trading for a Living

# 4

# Serving investors

## Sustaining losers

Investors are the readers we think we understand best. From business news pages to corporate websites, from press releases to dot.coms, we write the most of all for this audience alone. Yet it remains terribly ill-served. How do we know? Because share prices rise and fall, stock markets soar and crash, and small investors, who rely most heavily upon newspapers and online services for their investment decisions, consistently lose money to professionals, who have access to better quality research.[1]

> **Adults in the developed world wear the trappings of financial sophisticates.**

There is ample scope for better business reporting. But to understand how to serve these news consumers better, we need to understand their investment behaviour, and see where the information flow is failing. Who are they, and what is it they need from us?

## The spread of shareholding

Adults in the developed world wear the trappings of financial sophisticates. In Chapter 1 we looked at the breadth of the shareholder culture in the USA, but the story is no different in Europe. In the UK, three-quarters of adults invest, often in complex products.[2] Ten years ago, the savings account was the backbone of the personal investment industry. Today, it's an old-fashioned haven left behind in the rush into pensions, unit and investment trusts, and shares, where the returns are (supposedly) better. (See chart below.)

Knowledge about finance may be thinly spread, but who doesn't wish they'd invested £1,000 in Glaxo Wellcome shares 20 years ago, for a return of £15.7 million? In a Nationwide savings account the same investment delivered £3,720.[3]

The British have also been very busy collecting bonuses. Some have come as windfalls as the building societies and other mutually-owned organizations have changed status, others have been dished out as employee share options or profit-related share bonuses. Consequently, at the turn of the millennium 40 per cent of British adults owned shares – either directly or through trusts.[4] That's a greater proportion of the population than ever before, and a spread that spans both income and social class. The majority

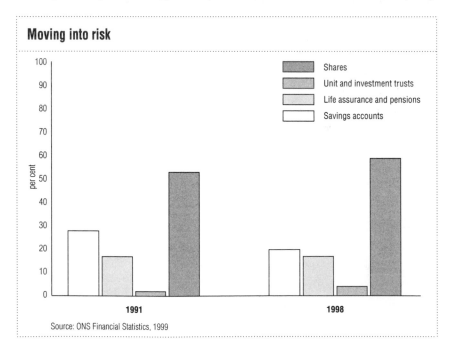

**Moving into risk**

Shares
Unit and investment trusts
Life assurance and pensions
Savings accounts

per cent

1991          1998

Source: ONS Financial Statistics, 1999

of people who own their houses also own shares, but so too do 8 per cent of those who rent from local authorities or housing associations.[5]

Similarly, most full-time employed and self-employed own shares. But shares are also widely owned by part-timers, the retired, family carers, the sick or disabled and even the unemployed. In 1999, 15 per cent of Britons earning less than £5,999 a year owned shares.[6]

The shareholders that really trade, rather than just sitting on a one-off holding, are just as diverse[7]. In fact, the only things that British shareholders do have in common these days are their age (three-quarters are over 35), their marital status (three-quarters are married rather than single or divorced), and their inadequate understanding of the stock market.[8] Very few understand the most basic elements of corporate finance, let alone the relationship between a company's profits and its share price. But then, the majority are new to share ownership (see box opposite and above). [9]

| Personal shareholders – 1998 | |
|---|---|
| As a percentage of the adult population | |
| | % |
| Sweden | 53 |
| USA | 40 |
| Denmark | 33 |
| Australia | 32 |
| UK | 27 |
| Russia | 27 |
| Canada | 25 |
| Ireland | 20 |
| Finland | 19 |
| Switzerland | 13 |
| France | 10 |
| Japan | 9 |
| Norway | 8 |
| Germany | 6 |
| Netherlands | 6 |
| Belgium | 5 |
| Austria | 4 |
| India | 2 |

Sources: Proshare – citing AKTIENFORUM, Vienna 1998; *The Financial Times*, 2 Feb. 1999, MORI Analysis, and the NYSE and the Irish Stock Exchange

## Shareholders as readers

As an audience, readers about the stock market split three ways. First come the active investors. In the UK, these make up a third of the nation's 12.5 million private shareholders.[10] They strike more than 35,000 deals a day worth £320m, accounting for more than half of the London Stock

Exchange (LSE) deals and a substantial proportion of brokers fees and commissions. But they trade in tiny bundles. All this dealing still only accounts for 7 per cent of the LSE's total trade. Small investors are simply drowned in volume by the large institutions.

**The private shareholders who trade are losers. They act with too little information, and too little understanding.**

But not so when it comes to information. Then a small trade is every bit as demanding as a large one. Investors need to assess risks and opportunities whether they are backing their findings with £1,000 or £1m: and for the 1.5 million British shareholders who trade at least six times a year, not to say the quarter-million who trade more than 16 times a year, this research has to be a near constant process.[11]

Then come the two-thirds who have never traded. Monitoring the shares they own is part of their interest. But many are also 'wannabe' buyers and sellers, who lack the know-how. They divide evenly over whether they use the media or an Independent Financial Adviser to find out how to trade (far fewer turn to brokers).[12]

Finally, come the non-shareholders, who on the face of it have no need to follow the markets. The market affects these readers, whether they know it or not, through their pensions, life assurance and even insurance bills (see box opposite), which is why stock market crashes halt economies. There are very few people who don't lose when the stock market dives. So spare a thought for those on the sidelines. They too need journalists to make the links between the market's behaviour and the things they are doing, or want to do.

## ▶ A catalogue of irrational behaviour

The private shareholders who trade are losers. Consistently, and across all market conditions, they transfer wealth to professional investors, and to the investment industry in fees and trading costs, because they act with too little information, and too little understanding. The following mistakes are close to universal.[13]

## Public shares – who owns them***

As a percentage of total shares owned in 1998

|        | Individuals | Insurance companies | Pension funds | Overseas holders |
|--------|-------------|---------------------|---------------|------------------|
| UK     | 16.5        | 23.5                | 22.1          | 24               |
| USA    | 41.9        | 6                   | 24            | 7.3              |

|           | | Individuals | Financial companies** | Overseas holders |
|-----------|--|-------------|------------------------|------------------|
| France    | 32.1 | 23     | 22.1 | |
| Spain*    | 28.7 | 22.8   | 37.3 | |
| Italy     | 25.8 | 22.2   | 6.6  | |
| Germany*  | 16.8 | 37.2   | 12.2 | |
| Sweden*   | 15   | 30.5   | 31.7 | |

Notes

*1997 figures
** Pensions, insurance, banks and financial institutions
*** Calculation methods vary across these countries
Sources: ONS Share Ownership, US Federal Reserve Board and Federation of European Stock Exchanges – all as cited by Proshare

## The future

Investment is about future returns – yet small investors, no matter how experienced, expect the future to be an extrapolation of the past. If a stock is doing well now, they expect it to perform well in the future.[14] This is not a good platform to start from. Share prices hardly ever just keep going the same way.

You need to highlight the elements that mean the future will **not** be the same as the past, and give the context that enables readers to draw the implications of these changes.

## The reputation

Private investors buy shares on the basis of a company's profile or reputation, rather than its potential as an investment. They also like familiarity, which means they buy household names. The very fact that these stocks act as a magnet to small investors means they deliver relatively low returns, because they are overvalued. (See box overleaf.)

> ### Keeping poor performers in funds
>
> ◆ Private investors choose which funds to invest in on the basis of recent returns – they virtually ignore the different levels of risk and administration costs.
>
> ◆ If returns plummet, they don't pull out.
>
> ◆ This has seen funds left holding millions of dollars of consumers' money even *after* losses of more than 25 per cent a year for eight years.
>
> Source: See Note 15

You need to structure stories around investment criteria. Spell out the current returns on an investment. In comments, emphasize the strengths and weaknesses of a share as a future earner. And remember: you are not writing stories about companies in good or bad shape, but stories about shares that are under or overvalued on the basis of a company's potential for growth.

## The spread

Amateur investors own shares in very few companies. Yet all the evidence shows that a broader portfolio increases returns and reduces risk (hence the appeal of investment funds).

You need to start thinking in terms of diversity. Don't just write stories about companies and sectors – write about portfolios too. What makes a good mix, what is complementary, how are (successful) fund managers structuring their holdings? Portfolio mix barely gets a mention in the current offerings to investors – yet it's the key to solid returns.

## The buy

Although less informed than the professionals, small investors are *no* less confident as buyers, because they over-estimate the quality of their information. They nearly always pay too much for shares – having only become aware of potential *after* the price has adjusted to reflect the anticipated growth. They are also over-optimistic about the performance of the companies they are in.

## The sale

Individual shareholders cash in gains, but leave losses to accumulate. It's easy to understand why. If you'd made 20 per cent on a share, selling to realize your gain would seem a nice, sensible, risk-averse thing to do. With losses, the hope is that given long enough things will improve and they will turn into gains. But the sum of this strategy is that investors stay in poor performers. Selling winners and holding losers sees them locking into low returns. In fact, what investors keep and what they sell should never be dictated by losses and gains, but by the future outlook for the share (or fund).

> ❝ Cut the weeds and cultivate the flowers. It's sound advice … but tell [an investor] that there is a metaphorical dandelion in their portfolio … and they will claim it is really a rose ❞
>
> *Investors Chronicle*

## The correction

Once investors understand their information disadvantage, they change their behaviour. They stop falling into the traps of naïve and overly aggressive share trading, and start making money.[16]

It really is important that you are writing about investment behaviour and strategies. Highlight the traps, **and provide more information of the quality available to professionals.**

# ▶ The information gap

Delivering edited highlights from company press releases is not enough. You may think you've covered all bases if you give the sales and profits

**Delivering edited highlights from company press releases is not enough.**

figures, an executive's quote on why they are what they are, and perhaps a smattering of other financials. But where does this cocktail leave the small investor?

It's nothing but a skim over the top that feels like enough to inform a decision, but isn't, which makes it a con of the first order. People only buy financial news because they believe it will make them better off. Giving the reader the sense he is informed, without relaying the critical elements, leaves him worse off than if he'd read nothing. Without any information he wouldn't trade. On the basis of a skim, he'll trade and lose.

So you need to develop a new way of thinking: think change, think future and think valuation. We only care one iota about any announcement because of what it tells us about **prospects.** We don't deliver it as the companies normally do – without context. Disposals and acquisitions are tele-

> ### Professional advantage
>
> ◆ The professionals specialize by sector.
>
> ◆ They have access to companies' senior management.
>
> ◆ They receive trade journals and trade and financial databases.
>
> ◆ They talk constantly to middle management, industry consultants and other specialists.
>
> ◆ Companies care about their goodwill.

phone numbers unless we get some industrial logic. If a company's pitching into a new market, tell readers about that market. If it has changed the way it works get to grips with the gains this might genuinely deliver – we don't care about the gloss. These are real live businesses that are developing as we write – which way, and how fast? Wean yourself off the announcements and away from the multinationals, and do the public a favour: go expose some dogs or darlings.

While you're out there, try opening the door on the professionals (see box) – let's see what fund managers do, who they are, how they spend their mid-afternoons. What do they talk about, think and wonder? How do they balance their holdings? What works, and what doesn't? These huge investors are as important to the returns your readers make as the companies they back, because it's the funds that drive the markets.

## The new perils of trading

If someone buys a clutch of shares, and sits on them for decades, they are almost certain to end up ahead compared with almost any other way of investing. The same sums don't work if they start trading. Yet everything is pointing to the increased involvement of small shareholders in buying and selling, not least the advent of online trading.

**By the end of 1999, online trading was drawing 35 per cent of private shareholder business in the USA.**

By the end of 1999, online trading was drawing 35 per cent of private shareholder business in the USA. The same climb had begun in Europe, with Paris reporting a rise in online trading from almost nothing to 15 per cent of stock exchange business and J.P. Morgan forecasting 8.3 million online trades a year in Europe by 2002.[17]

The scurry to hook private traders in this new, competitive market is bringing down fees and changing information services. As brokers' sites branch out into news analysis and comment, and news services incorporate trading facilities, the two types of services are converging, which is making investment easier.

However, the effects of online trading are not all positive. It is also opening the door to some of the biggest investment gaffes yet, as amateurs move into day trading. There have always been traders – people who profit from price movements caused by mismatches between the supply and demand for particular shares.[18] But, until now, these people were professionals. Online trading has changed that – in the USA, and increasingly in Europe, private investors are piling into the most fickle of markets. For them, information about a company's future performance is irrelevant – they may only hold the stock for seconds. The trigger for a purchase is likely to be a rumour, or a price movement begun that they hope will go farther.

## A word on bonds

- More money is tied up in bonds than shares.

- Bonds are the debt of a company, government, local authority or even a mortgage lender.

- Bond prices are dictated by interest rates, and the credit rating of the borrower.

- Borrowers' ratings change to reflect greater or lesser degrees of risk.

- Small investors own 12 per cent of US bonds.

## The establishment view

**On-line trading may be quick and easy; on-line investing – and I emphasise investing – requires the same old-fashioned elbow grease like researching a company or making the time to appreciate the level of risk**

Arthur Levitt, Chairman of the Securities and Exchange Commission of the USA, addressing the National Press Club in May 1999

This chasing of momentary movements has not endeared the day trader to the financial establishment. Viewed as glamorous by some, they are more often scorned as gamblers and fly-by-nights whose trading only adds to meaningless share price volatility. There is also a problem in terms of day traders' losses.

Day trading is, in fact, rarely a source of great riches. The handful of studies to date all conclude that after fees and commissions day traders earn no more than regular investors, and often less. And many end up big losers. In the USA, one such trader even went on a killing rampage when his losses became too much to bear – bringing to a head the general concern at the rise in this new form of gambling. Nonetheless, there *are* news services that have been launched to service this audience. It's hard to see where the scope exists – day traders only want price data information on modelling techniques and access to day trader chat lines. There isn't much that business writers can do to tell them where prices are headed in the next hour!

## ▶ … and the old peril of sentiment

The stock market is a tale of two cities. Constant and rather still are the vast majority of investors. Oscillating frantically around this core are those who trade in and out to make a fast buck. Investors *follow* fundamentals – like whether a company is profitable and growing. The rapid traders *lead* sentiment, that is, the sum of all the price changes we cannot explain and are not logical. Sentiment can make a bigger difference to a small investor's returns than any amount of wisdom in backing companies with strong growth prospects.

**The stock market is a tale of two cities.**

For example, look at the calculation in the box opposite, courtesy of ProShare. This shows if you'd invested in London for a full 11 years, your average annualized return would have been 14.8 per cent. But if you'd missed the market's best 40 days, because you'd sold shares and not yet bought replacements, you'd have cut your returns for the **whole decade** by two-thirds! This is why stock market investment is risky. It's risky, even after we've got to grips with the nature of the companies we're funding, because the timing of trading is a rogue element.

The professionals are just as vulnerable in this. Although, unlike the small investor, they devote considerable time and energy to the study of sentiment. The chartists seek to predict where the market is headed based on its movements in the past. Others use indicators of how confident (or wealthy) we're all feeling, from consumer demand to golf club membership. There are even traders who overtly or covertly look to the stars for pointers on the market's wanderings.

Clearly, none of this is hugely illuminating. But an acute awareness of the market's fickle nature *can* help in avoiding the worst of its excesses. We can't predict sentiment, not absolutely. We can't explain it, not fully. But we can do a little of both and something else: even when the market is behaving like quick-sand there remain patches of firmer ground. Investment writers pay little attention, as a rule, to the factors that make individual shares more or less volatile. But this is big news when it comes to deciding on an investment. If small investors are going to mix with the rapid traders, they should at least be told where the risks are the smallest.

### The cost of missing the highs

Annualized return on London stock market investment from end 1986 to end 1997

| | |
|---|---|
| No days missed: | 14.8% |
| Best 10 days missed: | 10.7% |
| Best 20 days missed: | 8.8% |
| Best 30 days missed: | 6.8% |
| Best 40 days missed: | 5.2% |

Source: ProShare

## The central role of the funds

The fund managers who control the majority of the world's share capital are short-term thinkers and short-term actors seeking short-term gains. Unlike private investors, their jobs and their bonuses rest on quarterly performance targets: a pressure that inclines them to panic in volatile markets.

**Target-driven fund managers don't just dump shares that are tumbling. They buy shares that are soaring.**

In one study for the American Finance Association, two US academics looked at the share price movements on every day that the market moved by more than 2 per cent between 1988 and 1995. Come climb or fall, stocks with high institutional ownership moved almost twice as much as those with low institutional ownership.[19] Those held largely by mutual funds (the US equivalent of investment funds) were the most volatile of all. A similar study in the Netherlands found exactly the same.

Target-driven fund managers don't just dump shares that are tumbling. They buy shares that are soaring – even when they know it doesn't make

## Following the fickle fundholder

UK individual shareholders are concentrated in the best-known and largest companies – Tesco, Sainsbury, Rolls-Royce, British Airways, BaeSystems, Glaxo Wellcome, ICI, Barclays and Lloyds TSB. If the funds pull out of these shares, individual shareholders really take a knock– as seen with ICI in 1998, Marks & Spencer in 1999 and almost all the rest of the blue chips in 2000. In 1998, ICI's share price fell by more than 50 per cent at a time when a single institutional investor was pulling out!

sense. An example is the dizzy surge of the internet stocks at the turn of the millennium. The most plausible explanation for this extraordinary departure from all norms of company valuation was the surge in funds being committed by the small private investor. As one sage observed at the time, a bull market (one that's going up) only ends when the last buyer has bought. The rise of the IT bubble coincided with a massive injection of new money into the markets by poorly-informed investors.

With online news services initially breathless about the latest crop of internet stocks, readers carried on buying long after the pundits had calmed. There is nothing new about this. One study of *Business Week*'s quite sober Inside Wall Street column found a single positive mention was enough to induce an abnormal share price rise that took up to six months to correct.[20] But the fundholders were in there too. Said one, in March 2000, 'you cannot justify not holding these [technology] stocks. If your job and your bonus are measured on how you are performing, you can't go on saying the emperor has no clothes forever'.[21] But you *can* sell at the very first sign of trouble!

Fund managers knew they were heading into dangerous territory for the sake of their bonuses – that's different from believing in the mirage. It makes for a rapid exit once the price rise halts. Which should have made concentrations in institutional ownership big news – these were, are and will continue to be the stocks where the risk is greatest!

Moreover, fund managers are often responsible for broad capital movements, a prime example being the rush into European shares in 1998 as funds pulled out of investments in Asia. With more than $5.5 trillion to invest, the US mutual fund industry is absolutely capable of making and breaking markets if it moves in concert.[22]

Even when acting alone, the buying and selling strategies of individual funds can move prices (see box above). It is not unknown for a company's share price to benefit more from a fund deciding to increase its investment in that sector than from a huge improvement in that company's profit outlook, which is why we need to be reporting – and explaining – buying and selling by the funds.

Market reporting that **explains** what's driving supply, demand, and price volatility, is far more valuable to investors than any summary of movements and rumours. The actions of the funds go a long way in explaining all three. So, report what they're doing: small shareholders need to know.

## Dragging the bad news out of companies

As a business writer you are not just a passive observer. Your actions move markets. Companies know that, which has made the drive to achieve shareholder value a tale with a sting. There was a time when shareholder value meant a great lunch on the day of the annual general meeting. Now it means running businesses so that the share price rises. To this end, companies are making managers buy shares – so that they win or lose as the share price rises or falls. Similarly, directors' bonuses are being delivered in shares, or as options to buy shares and employees are being given share bonuses in lieu of pay rises. Not surprisingly, they are all beginning to care a great deal about 'their' share price.

This means they are striving harder than ever before to keep the price rising and stop it falling, which is a mixed blessing. It has made companies do more to ensure that investors can get information. But it has also seen the content and means of delivery tilted firmly towards the aim of achieving a buoyant share price.

Did you know, for instance, that stock markets underreact to disappointing (or even outstanding) financial results, but overreact to a string of good news or bad news?[23]

Clearly, shareholders grasp a profit warning (which forewarns of disappointing results) as bad news, in a way they do not with poor results themselves. Indeed, 'our profits are going to be lower than expected' does have a different ring to 'we achieved profits of £3.2bn, which on an underlying basis represented growth of 4 per cent on last year'.

| The goodwill chief executives say is essential to success | |
|---|---|
| | % |
| Customers | 80 |
| Employees | 76 |
| Institutional investors | 40 |
| Brokers' analysts | 24 |
| Private investors | 21 |
| Business media | 17 |
| Local communities | 6 |
| MPs and local officials | 5 |

Source: MORI research, cited in the *Financial Times*, 2 February 2000

Technically, companies **must** announce any insight into forthcoming disappointments. In reality, what usually happens is that companies keep institutional investors and analysts informed of the minutiae and leave the small investor to find out through the journalist after the event – if at all.

This only reinforces how necessary it is for you to get to the heart of the numbers on results day. It's vital that you communicate the full import of results – good and bad – for future earnings. It's just as important that you highlight decisions by management not to tell shareholders about setbacks as soon as they were apparent. Why didn't we see a profit warning?

Similarly, where you're being treated to a string of good news be chary. Investigate the timing, necessity and motive for these announcements, and be willing to refer to a company's determination to enhance its share price. Companies will manipulate you if you let them – so don't.

Your role is to get the best possible handle on a company's growth prospects, regardless of what it does or does not announce. Because you are *the* research source for small investors. Which means that you simply must be drawing the implications of events; highlighting and comparing

| For financial glossary |
|---|
| www.investorwords.com |

returns; and linking the experiences of individual businesses with broader trends and flows.

We shall be looking at ways of doing all of these things in the coming chapters. So, be warned. When it comes to serving investors, it is no longer enough to find a world-weary broker in a pub corner, and report back with the word on the street. This job is for the analyst, educator and raconteur, in one.

# Notes

1 For a review of the literature on small investors' behaviour see: 'A portrait of the individual investor', Werner F.M. De Bondt, 1998, *European Economic Review*, 42, 831–844. For an example of investors' use of information sources see 'Mutual fund shareholders: characteristics, investor knowledge, and sources of information', Gordon J. Alexander, Jonathan D. Jones, Peter J. Nigro, 1998, *Financial Services Review*, 7, 301–306.

2 For information on investment buying, see Office of Fair Trading, *The Consumer Survey*, January 1998, Appendix 4 of Vulnerable Consumers and Financial Services.

3 Calculations made by Robert Winnett, *The Sunday Times*, May, 2000.

4 OFT, as 2.

5 OFT, as 2.

6 *BMRB/Mintel Survey*, November, 1998.

7 *MORI Analysis*, commissioned by ProShare and the London Stock Exchange; and *CPSO Share Ownership Survey*, 1996.

8 For examples of investors' financial literacy, see the Investor Knowledge Survey conducted for ITP by Princeton Survey Research Associates in 1996 (www.investorprotection.org/nrl.htm)

9 BMRB Target Group Index survey 1997–98, Mintel, November 1998.

10 *Shares and Share Ownership, Facts and Figures*, 4th edn, prepared by ProShare (UK) Ltd, April 1999. Note, this is a first-rate publication: a must for any UK investment writer.

11 Ibid 14.

12 Results of a survey of recipients in the 1997 windfall bonanza by MORI Financial Services commissioned by ProShare and the London Stock Exchange in April 1998. In fact, 22 per cent of respondents said they would use the media, compared with 24 per cent an Independent Financial Advisor and 11 per cent a broker, which puts financial news firmly in the running as a source for more than a million 'wannabe' share traders.

13 Ibid 3, see De Bondt.

14 For example, since 1989, the proportion of US investors who believe that a 3 per cent drop in the market one day will be followed by a rise the next day has risen from 1:1 in 1989 to 3:1 in 1999. Thus the belief that the market will keep rising is far greater at the end of a sustained period of rising share prices than it was when prices were more subdued. Investor confidence ratings cited by Robert Shiller in the *Financial Times*, April 2000. www.ft.com

15 'Investor behaviour and the persistence of poorly-performing mutual funds', David W. Harless and Steven P. Peterson, 1998, *Journal of Economic Behaviour & Organization*, 37 (3), 257–276.

16 'Confidence and the welfare of less-informed investors', Robert Bloomfield, Robert Libby and Mark W. Nelson, 1999, *Accounting, Organizations and Society*, 24, 623–647.

17 Figures cited by Association Brokers On-Line, France. Paris press conference 19 January 2000.

18 Thanks for this definition to Michael Griffis, *In Stocks Today*, 19 April 1999, www.stocks.about.com

19 'Professional money managers panic most in volatile markets', Deon Strickland and Patrick Dennis, presentation to the American Finance Association, January 2000.

20 Market reaction to *Business Week* 'Inside Wall Street' column: 'A self-fulfilling prophecy', Rajiv Sant and Mir A. Zaman, 1996, *Journal of Banking & Finance*, 20 (4), 617–643.

21 David Rough of Legal & General, quoted in *The Observer*.

22 Bond Market Association, www.bondmarkets.com or www.investinginbonds.com

23 For a review of the empirical findings on shareholders' reactions to different kinds of announcements, see 'A model of investment sentiment', Nicholas Barberis, Andrei Shleifer and Robert Vishny, 1998, *Journal of Financial Economics*, 49 (3), 307–343.

**❝Drill for oil?**
**You mean drill into the**
**ground to try to find oil?**
**You're crazy❞**

Drillers to Edwin L. Drake in 1859

# 5

# Frontier reporting

## ▶ Reaching entrepreneurs

The owners and financiers of small businesses drive our economies. They create most new jobs. They control the majority of the world's wealth Their choices about what businesses they launch dictate the direction of our economic growth. Yet their progress is hindered at every turn by their lack of information.

For business writers they represent the most peculiar of challenges. Managers know what information they want – the challenge for the writer is getting it to them. Investors know they want information, even if they don't know what information they need. But entrepreneurs don't even know that their problem is what they don't know. For the most part, information is simply not something they miss in their lives. And when there *is* something they'd like to know, they complain that it's hard to find. The diversity of their needs and the detail they need before data becomes useful, have put them off the media's map, except for the occasional feature about a guy who made it.

> Entrepreneurs don't even know that their problem is what they don't know. Information is simply not something they miss in their lives.

In this chapter, we shall look at the way entrepreneurs work, what information they actually do need, and how to get it to them in a form that they will buy, use and gain from.

## ▶ Why they matter

In the European Union there are 18 million businesses, excluding farms. Almost all of them are small or medium sized, and most are still owned, at least in part, by their founders or their founders' families.[1] The situation is not very different in the USA, where there are an estimated 11 million small businesses.[2]

This is a large audience: and one that is central to our economic prosperity. Smaller businesses produce more than half of Europe's total output and employ more than two-thirds of its workforce. It is the owners who decide when to start, or liquidate these businesses and when and how to shift activities, expand in new directions, buy up other businesses, or sell off parts of their own. Yet, the evidence is that most of these decisions are based on very little information. Most business activities are selected almost at random. People simply settle on a business they fancy – even in the world's most advanced enterprise culture, the USA. The result is a phenomenally high level of business failure. In the USA, 28 per cent of new businesses fail within their first three years, and 63 per cent within six years.[3]

> **Only three-quarters of the businesses that existed in the USA in 1992 were still in business by 1996.**

This brutal selection goes beyond eliminating those who select a duff line of business in the first place. It also knocks out potentially strong businesses that are poorly run. For while the chances of failure are higher for new businesses and for small businesses, companies of all sizes and all ages go under – regularly. So regularly that the face of business is changing radically all the time (see box above).

The scale of this ongoing failure (and renewal) makes the small business information market – as yet a largely unexplored territory – the most interesting of all. All business news is growing and evolving, but it is small business news that is set to move from nowhere to centre stage.

## ▶ The factors that stop them seeking information

Academics have spent decades trying to map the make-up of the entrepreneur. They haven't got far and even the broad categories are breaking down. More men than women start businesses, but women are catching up fast. Younger people, that is below 45, are more likely to launch businesses, but redundancies and early retirement have spurred start-ups among the over-50s.

> Most companies, even the largest, owe their existence to family money. *Reader's Digest* began with $5,000 from the family of founder deWitt. Walt Disney turned to Uncle Robert for the $500 that launched him into film.

The only clear marker is that people with money in the family are more likely to take the plunge.[4] In large part, this reflects the difficulty entrepreneurs have traditionally faced in raising start-up funds (see box). But secondary financial security also removes an important emotional barrier to starting a business: it is fear of financial ruin that keeps most of us from striking out alone. People from wealthy families tend to be less fearful about money evaporating.

On balance, people who start businesses *are* more optimistic than the rest of us.[5] Quite apart from anything else they all harbour an opening belief

**More men than women start businesses, but women are catching up fast.**

that their businesses won't ruin them, or, more positively put, that their businesses will flourish. This faith in the future makes a difference to the businesses they run. At the disastrous end, they run aground on cash-flow crises, unable to pay their bills, because they have been too ambitious with their spending – investing in too much too soon – and unduly confident about how quickly the company's income will grow.[6] For small companies this is the most frequent pattern of failure.

Optimism also affects their attitudes towards information (and record-keeping). The confident don't look to see if there is a seat behind them before they sit down. And entrepreneurs don't usually research their markets, or monitor their competitors. But this isn't just a matter of confidence. They also don't have time. Regardless of personality, mindset, age, gender or anything else, the one thing all entrepreneurs have in common is that they are trying to do what others do, with less.

## Their information needs

There are no dispensations for businesses just because they are small. No one forgives a lesser product and few of us are willing to pay a whole lot more. When someone starts a small business, they have to cover all bases.

### How small businesses learn

◆ They gossip, with customers, suppliers and competitors.

◆ They get trade association newsletters and magazines.

◆ They read direct mail advertising, newspapers and magazines.

Source: See Note 7

In a world of specialization, this makes entrepreneurs the multi-skilled – which is central to our understanding of their information needs – they do not want the information we think they want.

Distracted by their status as business *owners*, we are apt to overlook the fact that above all they are doing business (see box). The result of this trap is the small business news service that leads on 'how to get capital', and follows with 'budget office equipment' and 'taking on an employee'.

This is equivalent to telling a travelling sales rep how to buy a car and how to insure it, over and over and over again. It's fine for starters, but with his car bought and insured, his needs quickly move on to road maps, information about potential buyers and the low-down on marketing techniques.

The same is true for small business owners. Money and equipment is just a beginning. As loners in the big world of business, these readers are 20 specialists rolled into one. They buy and they market. They negotiate with customers, collect overdue invoices and keep up to date with technology. They recruit, pay and deduct tax from employees. They design the product or service, its presentation and the company image. Above all, they decide what to offer, and how best to sell it – and all without the supports normally pitched at specialists (see box opposite).

The owner of a three-person silk tie company isn't going to be attending the Paris conference on dealing with effluent from dying operations, or the Milan conference on next season's colours. She won't be visiting the packaging exhibition at Earl's Court, the marketing managers' seminar in Nice or even the book-keeping evening class at her local technical college. Possibly, she won't be touring too many Chinese silk farms either. She won't even be getting a trade publication that's giving her a second-hand shot at all of these forums. Her interests are too diverse. Trade publications don't just specialize, they play top-up to those who are already doing and knowing. A textiles publication doesn't run articles on accounting. Yet our silk tie wizard is only one-twentieth of an expert in anything.

This is why small businesses hit the problems they do. Take the list of headaches in the box overleaf. Many of these would not be problems if small businesses had access to the information and skills larger businesses take for granted.

Typical is the problem of attracting and retaining customers. It is common to the point of being a cliché for entrepreneurs to put together a great product, and then fail for no other reason than that few people ever know of the product's existence – marketing is something many neglect. Conversely, there are some that move into full sales gear, with a product that has really not got what it takes to win a market. The point is that small business owners are frequently managing alone, which means that their blind spots or weaknesses become the failings of the companies they run. For you, the writer, the challenge is to start filling these holes, with specialist information for a non-specialist audience.

> **Small businesses want to know about...**
>
> 1 Their specific industry.
> 2 Insurance regulations.
> 3 Safety issues.
> 4 Financial management.
> 5 Pending laws and taxes.
> 6 Production techniques.
> 7 IT solutions.
>
> Source: Edward Lowe Foundation, *1995 Survey of Entrepreneurs' Information Needs*

**It is common for entrepreneurs to put together a great product, and then fail for no other reason than that few people ever know of the product's existence.**

## ▶ Dealing with diversity

Imagine a news service that really did cover every base for the small business: industry after industry, sector after sector, markets, marketing, sourcing, production, legislation. Until recently, it was not a possibility. No one would wade through a newspaper with so much in it that was irrelevant to their lives. Media went for breadth, concentrating on articles that appealed to the widest possible audience, or depth, focusing on a narrow subject range. Neither format has served small businesses well. Broad coverage produces little that is really useful, and narrow coverage has typically presumed a formidable knowledge base and set aside context almost completely.

| Small business headaches | |
| --- | --- |
| | % |
| Labour shortages | 23 |
| Economic conditions in the USA | 16 |
| Cash flow | 9 |
| Attracting and retaining customers | 9 |
| Government regulations | 7 |
| Availability of financing | 6 |
| High taxes | 5 |
| Domestic competition | 5 |
| Economic problems in other countries | 2 |
| Expanding facilities | 2 |
| Rising costs | 2 |
| Keeping up with technology | 2 |
| Rising wages | 2 |

Source: Survey of US businesses, conducted for American City Business Journals, February 1999, www.amcity.com/madway/survey_1999/

Online services, however, are not bound by the same constraints as the old media. They are not limited by the problems of excess volume, which leaves them able to produce accessible depth across dozens of parallel fields. This kind of content doesn't age in a day, or even a month. Once in place, we can just keep developing it, rather than rebuilding it anew every 24 hours. So where do we begin for these business people who have been left on the outside?

## Delivering winning content

Markets maketh the business. No business can survive without its customers. Take a look at the selection, in the box opposite, of the failures among *Fortune*'s most promising start-ups.[8] All were grounded by the absence of a market.

Small businesses are almost always in the dark about their markets. An entire industry services larger companies with market research. But entrepreneurs can't pay the prices, which is why they get wedded to a single idea, and stick with it even when it isn't working.

They are not just being cussed. If you were running a college bookshop and the till receipts were down, what would you do about it? You could extend your opening hours, or offer coffee to browsers. But maybe you just have the wrong books. The first step to better market information might be contacting the lecturers and finding out what books they're recommending. That may help. But suppose you've done that, and sales are still down. Try this news: lecturers aren't just recommending books, they're putting internet sources on the reading lists. These are free and students anyway prefer working on their computers. Moreover, the student budget isn't what it used to be: suppose you got a sight of how far their money is having to stretch and it was fairly clear it didn't add up to many books per head. Now you know you've got a market problem that sitting it out won't solve. You are going to *have* to diversify.

Successful businesses have to evolve if they are to chase lucrative markets. Almost all of Europe's very large businesses expanded by changing activities. Glaxo Wellcome, one of the world's largest pharmaceutical companies, began as a producer of baby milk. ICI (and thus its offspring Zeneca, now merged with Astra) can be traced back to the salt mines of northern England. The willingness to move off in new directions has been the factor that has marked out the great from the rest.

Market information tells us where the dead ends are, and the most promising

## Missing the market

**AER Energy Res**. Couldn't persuade laptop makers to buy its special zinc air batteries, but lost $54.5m trying.

**C-Phone**. Lost a lot of money trying to market videophones.

**DaVinci**. Planned to make content for interactive television, but television didn't go interactive in time.

**Industry.net**. Ex-Lotus CEO's vision of a business-to-business web marketplace lost the race to another.

**Norris Comm**. Won only one big customer for its digital recording equipment – not enough to stem the losses.

**Thinking Mach**. Its 'massively parallel supercomputers' ended in Chapter 11 bankruptcy.

openings too. It can also help us to make what we have go further. Take differential pricing as an example. Goods and services fetch different prices in different places at different times and in different forms (because prices are dictated by many things other than what someone 10,000 miles away is willing to pay).

> Market information tells us where the dead ends are, and the most promising openings too.

The tourism market is typical. American tourists are willing to pay more than English tourists, who pay more than French tourists for the same hotel in the same place. Answer for the hotel owner: an advert in the *New York Times*. The art of supplying information to small businesses quickly comes down to recognizing when a very specific topic is going to have broad appeal. A piece on students' budgets and spending habits isn't only going to appeal to a bookshop owner. A piece on the prices tourists are willing to pay isn't just going to help one hotel.

> **Designing a company website?**
>
> ◆ What information do your small business customers need?
>
> ◆ Could you hook them with content: market research on their end market, technological blueprints for their processes, online seminars in marketing and packaging?
>
> ◆ Identify an information service that customers will flock to and your site will work a lot harder *for* you.

In reality, this audience is not as hard to serve as we think it is, nor even as disparate. Be it distribution methods, response rates to advertising, the men's fashion market, the demand for consultancy services, or the production of online content: we only need to unwrap these subjects to let owners pick them over (see box).

At the core of this news lie people's buying habits, business know-how, growth sectors and high-return activities, but anything is on the menu if it helps small businesses breach the hole left by the management team that other businesses have and they don't. What we're offering are short-cuts to experience – because business failures peak twice, once at start-up, and **again** at the handover to the next generation.

**We are opening a whole new ball game too, and that's writing for the non-business reader.**

Our role is to upgrade the capacity of those in business. But by moving hard and fast into business writing for the non-specialist, we are opening a whole new ball game too, and that's writing for the non-business reader.

## ▶ Opening a door to aspirants

How do you interest people in business, when they see it as an arcane game for insiders? You write about start-ups. The launch of new businesses is, quite simply, the portal into business for all. In the USA, more than a third of the population want to start their own business. Many others are interested in financing start-ups. And more again just want to look on as the winners win and the losers crumple.

On the story front, the start-up has it all: glamour, suspense, the promise of riches. And it's easy to understand. A business launch isn't steeped in the financial complexity of the money or futures markets. A brand new

**In the USA, more than a third of the population want to start their own business.**

company isn't running eight divisions in 32 countries with layers of cross-related hierarchies and functions. It's an idea that bankers and owners are backing, and viewers can comprehend. It's the business, by and large, of amateurs, which makes it a gift to business news services. Yet we're barely writing about it.

---

## A taste of start-up mythology

'This "telephone" has too many shortcomings to be seriously considered as a means of communication. The device is inherently of no value to us.'

Western Union internal memo, 1876

'Who the hell wants to hear actors talk?'

Harry M. Warner, Warner Brothers, 1927

'The concept is interesting and well-formed, but in order to earn better than a "C", the idea must be feasible.'

A Yale University management professor on Fred Smith's paper proposing an overnight delivery service. Smith went on to found Federal Express

'There is no reason for any individual to have a computer in their home.'

Kenneth Olsen, founder of Digital Equipment, 1977

'So we went to Atari and said, "Hey, we've got this amazing thing, even built with some of your parts, and what do you think about funding us? Or we'll give it to you. We just want to do it. Pay our salary, we'll come work for you." And they said, "No." So then we went to Hewlett-Packard, and they said, "Hey, we don't need you. You haven't got through college yet."'

Founders of Apple Computer talking about the personal computer

'If I had thought about it, I wouldn't have done the experiment. The literature was full of examples that said you can't do this.'

Spencer Silver on the work that led to the adhesives for 3-M "Post-It" Notepads

Thanks to Peter Cochrane, www.labs.bt.com/people/cochrane/quotes.htm

---

## ▶ Feeding dreams

Start-up legends make gripping copy. They have that David and Goliath angle that always hooks us as we strive in a world where so many things are so large. Just logging the resistance that our adventurers have overcome in delivering everyday commodities lifts our hearts (try it, see the box on previous page).

Indeed, myths are the bedrock of any enterprise culture. Germany's record in spawning manufacturing start-ups is absolutely tied in with the preponderance of industrial museums celebrating entrepreneurs past. A history of achievement expands our ideas about what is possible. And at base, most people don't start businesses because they don't believe they can. They may dream about it, but it remains outside their reality. Yet there is so much that we can do as business writers to expand their reality.

A classic model is the way the media has homed in on DIY. From television that transforms real homes, to newspaper style sections and interior design magazines, widespread coverage has expanded our interest, our ambitions and our belief in our own capacity to tackle skilled projects. The same is just as possible for business. TV can take people's business ideas, and launch them, at speed: the money, the premises, the packaging. It can run gurus' programmes, which go into people's lives and devise *the* businesses for them to run – turning the garage into an asset we wouldn't have imagined.

Similarly, the local media has a chance to jump-start local economies. Take my home town, which has not flourished in recent years. Exmouth, in Devon, wears the air of decline so typical of British seaside resorts. In the town centre, once filled with every kind of commercial venture, life has shrunk. The town has twice the population it did two decades ago, but at its centre there are now just building societies and charity shops.

If a local newspaper started gathering and printing the market information and business know-how that are the lifeblood of small businesses it could be so different. What would readers like to buy locally? What skills do they have? What ideas do they have? It's not hard to run telephone polls and publish the results (and people do love to read polls in which they and their neighbours figure). There's a chance, too, to combine national information on viability with local circumstance and ambitions.

If you were reading in your local paper about carpenters elsewhere earning £50 an hour making four-poster beds, and businesses clearing £100,000 a year in profits offering outsourced farm management, it would build a growing sense of what works and what might work here. Wouldn't you have a small think about whether these were things you could do too? Even the positioning in a local paper or website makes the subject more accessible. And there can be no doubt that vibrant writing about local business stands up well in the ratings compared with the local hockey league.

For the national press, there's the start-up reckoner. We could get personal about this, and start offering a for-publication service assessing the strengths and weaknesses of that start-up plan.

These are only ideas. The next few years will deliver many more, and far better. But the point is that we are missing a trick here. Running businesses is like running lives. If we think we know how to write about people then we *can* open the door on this great adventure, and draw whole new audiences along the way.

And there is every reason to do it. At the grandest level, it will make economies sing, and for our own information businesses, it's a commercial necessity. These are competitive times in the information market and small business is the new glamour. In the USA, one survey of baby boomers found 13 per cent already had their own businesses. That is, 13 per cent and rising. If we want to attract younger audiences, we too have to be at the frontier.

## ▶ News from the frontier

There can be no enterprise culture until we're all reading and talking about business, which means developing business frontier reporting in the mainstream. What follows are some of the formats we are going to be seeing a lot more of over the next few years.

### All the rage

New business goes through fashions, which means we should be writing about gold rushes, little and large. Be it Asian manufacturing, French gîtes, online news, or in-line skates, when everyone rushes in the profits

## No golden eggs here

When chicken battery farms became the "fab" business in Kenya in the early 1990s, no one wrote about the supply and demand for eggs. No one investigated the myth of good money in chickens. There were no stories about returns, profitability, start-up rates, or industrial prospects. Only when the egg glut hit, did the news hounds scramble.

disappear, which makes gold-rush news more than the flagging of an opportunity: it's *the answer* to over-investment. We should be watching start-up statistics, quizzing small business financiers, and running pieces about where and why the wonder businesses are, and how profitable they are really proving (see box).

## Spotting needs

Clever businesses spot needs. Their strength lies in serving a need we didn't even know we had, like Petplan, which devised an insurance plan against the risk of a huge vet's bill. So, next time you hear of any kind of personal or business difficulty, run a check – is this something many people face and is there a conceivable product or service that could offer up a solution? Indeed, you don't even have to conceive a solution. If this is something that many people face, write it as a business news story. This is a market, and it's unfulfilled – at what cost?

> There can be no enterprise culture until we're all reading and talking about business.

## Heading for growth

We need to start finding out where the best profits are being made. But there's no need to hunt. Set up a feature slot that showcases companies with operating profits and return on capital employed (see Chapter 10) of greater than 35 per cent, and free publicity is the incentive that'll bring the real superstars out from under cover. It's kudos for the companies, and addictive for the roving reader.

## Next generation

Don't just write about technology, IT or anything else that's going to change the face of an industry. Draw the implications in next generation reporting. The *Tomorrow's World* television show is a format we all love, so apply it.

## Human tales

Have you ever read a story about one of the people who has gone for a gold rush? Not a movie, or a throwaway line about John, who found a diamond the size of his fist. But what it cost, why he did it, how it played. People have real live experiences at the frontiers, and we're all armchair travelers now.

## Frontier without frontiers

Remember, this is a frontier without frontiers. A readership survey by FT.com in December 1999 found people using the site in more than 100 countries, including Antarctica, Azerbaijan, Uzbekistan and Qatar. When you write that piece on the pollution-free car, you won't just be drawing local readers as you spell out the opportunity.

# ▶ The private investor audience

Start-ups *are* a route to riches. Of those that survive, half become impressively profitable. Which is the final reason why start-ups are business news dynamite. For a new audience of funders, they are proving irresistible.

Private investors in the USA are now investing more than $20bn a year in the small and the young.[9] They would invest more – 35 per cent more according to one study – if they could find the opportunities. In Europe and Asia, these business angels are less common, but their ranks are growing. In the UK, there are now an estimated 18,000 individuals investing around £500m a year in 3500 companies.[10]

> **Profile of an American angel**
>
> The "average" US angel is 47 years old, has an annual income of $90,000, a net worth of $750,000, is college educated, has been self-employed, and invests $37,000 per venture. Most invest within 50 miles of home. They expect an average return on their capital of 26 per cent a year. This average includes the one-third of investments that produce a substantial capital loss.
>
> Source: See Note 11

All are high-risk investors; more than three-quarters of companies that fail return nothing to unsecured creditors and shareholders. Yet as the first financial backers of the computer industry, the biotechnology industry and most lately the internet industry, they are changing the world. Go back a century, and they even had a hand in the advent of the car (see box overleaf ).

### Angel legends

In 1903, five angels invested $40,000 in a car business: the entrepreneur was Henry Ford.

At the end of the 1970s, small investors financed the stage show CATS with shares priced at £750. They have since made more than £25,000 a share.

This is why angel investment is now firmly on the official map: rarely a budget or a policy review goes by without fresh incentives for angel investors. Typical is the UK's Enterprise Incentive Scheme, which makes returns on small business investments tax exempt, and offers income and capital gains tax incentives to boot. The rise of the angel is also spawning a rash of finance 'dating agencies', matching businesses and investors. Which leaves the new funders seeking only the information and skills to sift the winners from the losers: **from you**.

However, angels invest only small amounts of money each – an average of £57,000 a time in the UK.[12] Companies looking for more go to seed or venture capitalists, and this is a growth industry too. These funds buy into small companies with the aim of helping manage them into becoming much larger. The funds then sell out to investors with less of a taste for risk – typically by going for a stock exchange listing.

On the face of it, this type of finance should be less risky than the fare of the angels. Venture capitalists tend to come in slightly later in a company's life. But these funds do little better than the private investors, ending up with a third or more of their investments in duds. According to one

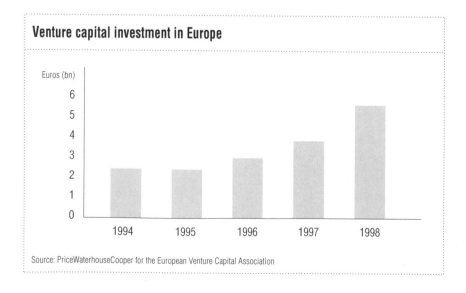

**Venture capital investment in Europe**

Euros (bn)

Source: PriceWaterhouseCooper for the European Venture Capital Association

Harvard professor, private equity funds as a whole (that is, including later-stage private investment, which is typically less risky) made an annual average return of just 17.1 per cent in the 20 years to 1999. This is less than a private individual could have made by investing in public companies through the stock exchange. Nonetheless, this level of return continues to be high enough to attract ever more funds. Indeed, so keen are US venture capitalists to increase their investments that they have been piling into Europe in search of fresh opportunities (see graph opposite).

Just like the angels, venture capitalists are running out of companies to invest in. Which is why the information industry really needs to kick in hard. Our economies have the capital – all we need is the knowledge to press **Go**.

## Notes

1 Eurostat, Statistics in Focus, Industry, Trade and Services, no. 3, 1999, www.eubusiness.com/employ/990310es.htm

2 Small Business Administration, www.sba.gov/ADVO/stats/answer.html

3 Ibid 2.

4 'What makes an entrepreneur? Evidence on inheritances and capital constraints', David Blanchflower and Andrew Oswald, 1998, *Journal of Labor Economics*, 16 (1).

5 See J.A. Carland, and J.W. Carland, 1992, 'Managers, small business owners and entrepreneurs: The cognitive dimension', *Journal of Business and Entrepreneurship*, 4 (2), 55–56.

6 'And a vision appeared unto them of a great profit: evidence of self deception among the self-employed', Gholamreza Arabsheibani, David de Meza, John Maloney, Bernard Pearson, *Economic Letters*, 67 (1), 35 –41.

7 *How Small Businesses Learn*, Sydelle Raffe, Eric Sloan, Mary Vencill, 1994, a study undertaken for the US Small Business Administration (www.sba.gov)

8 Cool Companies 1998: 'The coolness factor Part 2', Julie Creswell, 1998, *Fortune*, 6 July www.pathfinder.com/fortune/1998/980706/fiv1.htm

9 Estimates run as high as $50bn a year, but perhaps the most reliable is that of $27bn from a study commissioned by the US Small Business Administration, published in Robert Gaston, 1989, *Finding Private Venture Capital for Your Firm*, Wiley, Chichester.

10 www.nationalbusangels.co.uk

11 Various, including research by William Wetzel, Director of the Center for Venture Research, University of New Hampshire; Bill Cate's *Equity Finance Solutions* newsletter at mailto.money'southcoast.com; and also see findingmoney.com/investors.html

12 Ibid 10.

‘When something
	important is going on,
silence is a lie’

A.M. Rosenthal

# 6

# Getting to the truth

## ▶ If it's hidden, we want it

The control of information in business news is rarely a matter of shredded files, illegal operations and law courts. It's an everyday reality of people hiding things they don't want us to write about. You can see why it happens. When we write something negative, we wave a red flag to investors and consumers. Deliver positive news and we are giving someone somewhere a plug not shared by peers and rivals. It's not surprising everybody wants to be a winner from press coverage – and no one a loser. But if we go down the path of always trying to please those we write about, we abuse the single loyalty that matters – the welfare of our readers.

> Serving our audience means telling it like it is, and to do that we need to find out what is being hidden.

Serving our audience means telling it like it is, and to do that we need to find out what is being hidden, which is why this chapter is going to look in some detail at the strategies for control, their effectiveness, and how they can be countered.

## ▶ Because information *is* power

Business and inside information go hand in hand. Wherever people are making money, information is gleaned, gathered and guarded.

## Control through censorship

For details of the legislation that can get us into trouble for what we write, see www.indexoncensorship.org

The index on the same site gives a summary of recent penalties, and the stories that have prompted them, country by country. There's plenty of business news there.

Even the London Stock Exchange began as a cosy little information clique, as merchants, adventurers and investors met, struck deals and exchanged gossip in the coffee houses of the city of London. When the exchange went formal, and got a house of its own, the flow of information didn't change much. There were penny sheets – several were forerunners of today's *Financial Times*. But those 'in-the-know' were a select band. Indeed, until relatively recently, members of London's prestigious gentlemen's clubs could expect to have far better business information at their disposal than others, as they exchanged inside-track data over dinner. There can be no doubt some benefited materially from all this knowledge.

> 66 The individual with the information controls the business 99
>
> Finance Director
>
> Source: Reuters Business Information in Information as an Asset

In many emerging countries, real business information is still closely held. The clique with the knowledge may be former military classmates, members of a ruling family, or simply aspirants who have got plugged in. But the rule is that most people do not know what is going on, for most of the time, which is a sure and certain way of keeping power concentrated.

In the West, the bank of information held back from the public is dwindling. But there are still plenty of reasons for keeping secrets. Private information may be the key to competitive advantage, or it may reveal that things are not as rosy (or even as legal) as they could be, which makes damage limitation (covering up) the order of the day.

Whatever the motives for economizing with the truth, the strategies of control are universal, which is why we are not going to look at the extraordinary harassment that can rain down on business journalists when the financial interests and even the liberty of the unscrupulous are threatened. Revealing secrets can put your life at risk. One former student of mine, whilst putting together a series of stories exposing the corruption of a Pakistani port authority, was left permanently scarred after a meeting with an inside source turned out to be a set-up that saw him chased and felled by a pair of motorcyclists. This is not normal. If you think this kind of harassment is in the offing, don't work alone and get advice about security. For the rest, here are some pointers on moving beyond the control that others will seek to exert over you.

## The art of collusion

Companies live or die by reputation, and writers purvey reputations. Which leads to plenty of friction as companies offer only good news, and journalists search for the hidden catch. In this conflict of interests, collusion is the most sophisticated, invidious and effective method of control you are likely to encounter.

Your success in getting the fullest possible picture depends significantly on the co-operation of the organization you're writing about. This dependence opens the door to the company trading information in exchange for control over what is published. Companies will normally give far more information when a journalist co-operates over the way in which he uses that information – and it is in the journalist's interest to write from a position of knowledge, even if he cannot share that knowledge

**In many emerging countries, real business information is still closely held, which is a sure and certain way of keeping power concentrated.**

This sets up a balancing act that dictates the quality and candour of almost all business news. But it also creates an increasing problem for journalists as they get closer to the companies they cover. At the *Financial Times*, where the majority of reporters cover specialist beats, it is normal practice to move journalists every two to three years, specifically to prevent them becoming too close to their sources. Inevitably, as relationships build, the degree of collusion grows, resulting in fantastically well-informed journalists, who feel constrained from passing on much of the information at their command.

You can understand the trap. Geoff at Beefcakes Ltd has just explained the company's acquisition intentions down to the finest detail, on the basis that this is just between yourselves. You now know the company's plans, which is a victory in itself, and does feel good. But if you write about them, or even hint at them in some cases, Geoff's neck will be on the block. He will consider your story a major breach of trust, your relationship will be worse than if you had been strangers, and by going farther than the rest of the media pack you will have, additionally, set up a credibility problem should a denial ensue. Inside and beyond your publication, scoops are lonely territory, as news editors and readers alike wonder how much they should trust this story from you, and only you. What's more, by committing yourself to secrecy, you've tied your hands should you subsequently get the information from elsewhere (which happens surprisingly often. Companies don't generally tell journalists things, even in secret, if no one else at all already knows).

In short, the more you collude the more you are pushed down the path of using your extensive knowledge as nothing more than a foil against errors. Indeed, the end point becomes the moment when you cede control over content completely. I recall one journalist who read back every story he wrote, in full, to every supplier of information, before passing it to the newsdesk.

At first sight, this might seem sensible. Surely it is better to be right in every detail. But ensuring that suppliers of information are *happy* with what you have written is not the same as being right. Even balance can hurt. Just suppose for a second that the subject of the news story was you. Are you sure that a candid assessment of your strengths and weaknesses might not be just a little bruising? When it gets to the point where we cannot risk offending those we write about, it's time to stop writing. Because readers aren't coming to us for advertising literature: we are the independents.

> When it gets to the point where we cannot risk offending those we write about, it's time to stop writing.

Collusion will inevitably be necessary in getting the best for your readers, but you should never lose sight of your purpose. You are not there to satisfy the vanity of executives, fulfill the whims of PR companies, or boost the share bonuses of directors. You are there to find out what the reader would like to know. Which means you collude in order to get more information to pass on, not less.

Don't settle for secrets that get your readers nowhere. Companies that won't give you information you can use are not worth cultivating for more of the same. They are not playing ball, and neither should you. If you cannot strike a reasonable compromise over what you can reveal, go with the story as you have it and leave the company to agonize over where its attempt to control backfired.

## The closed door

Collusion is the sophisticated way of exercising control over writers. The blunt alternative is to say nothing and hide everything. Where few people are affected by a business's actions and fortunes, this kind of retreat from public exposure amounts to a legitimate desire for privacy. But for companies that are owned by your readers, employ large numbers of them, or provide a product or service on which a substantial minority depend, information about their prospects is clearly in the public interest.

> **Playing national sensitivities**
>
> US companies hate to talk about market share – because the competition authorities are so tough. In the UK, companies don't give profit figures except where they absolutely have to by law – because the British don't like paying for profits. So, go to the US operation for the profit breakdown, and get market share from a UK press office. It often works.

> Collusion is the sophisticated way of exercising control over writers.

Yet often in these circumstances, journalists will be stonewalled. Indeed, some of the world's leading companies deliberately pursue a policy of obstruction, in the belief that this is the best way of controlling the press.

The saddest thing about such companies is that no one but the journalists ever gets to know which companies are horrors to deal with and which are a delight. Journalists hardly ever write about companies' PR strategies or records, despite being in a unique position to do so, and despite the obvious relevance to shareholders and others. There are many people who might wish to know when a company is actively seeking to prevent transparency of its operations.

Journalists do have some recourse through describing companies, in passing, as secretive, or publicity shy. This happens regularly enough, and normally means the company in question will do everything within their power to prevent journalists obtaining any information about them.

The belief that this kind of poor or obstructive information service amounts to an effective means of control is not entirely without substance.

## Breaking down the door

◆ Talk to customers, competitors, and middle management.

◆ Write often.

◆ Be revealing about the level of obstructiveness encountered.

◆ Never give up.

◆ Commission research.

There are hundreds of stories that never get written, because although the journalist suspects something to be the case, or even knows it to be so, he or she cannot substantiate it from an authoritative source.

However, the success, for companies, of a closed-door strategy does depend on knowing when to open it. Almost invariably, extremes of obstruction are counter-productive. A prime example of this is the oil group Shell, one of the world's largest companies – for many years it was the largest. Its powerful position may explain why Shell's press office acted solely as a gate-keeping operation, seeking to deter, rather than service. This defensive posture is not uncommon amongst large companies. But Shell's version was extreme. The press office number was apparently manned by phone answering machines, with no alternative number for urgent business. Return calls were rare, even after repeated messages. In the unusual event that a press officer did call back, there was scant possibility of obtaining any information, beyond being sent a fax of some pages from the company's by-then-aged annual report. All interviews were denied. And any other requests for information were classed as not possible to service.

Imagine then, the chain of events, when environmental groups started shooting out press releases about a soon-to-be-discarded North Sea oil rig owned by Shell. There was no possibility of getting a defence from the company. When the company did start issuing press releases on the subject it did so to an audience of journalists with whom it had no working relationship. Not only did they have no trust for the company's pronouncements, there was also considerable antipathy in place, based on years of frustration in the face of the company's high-handedness. The same was true when controversy over the company's involvement in Nigeria came to the fore. The ground for a bad press had been laid many times over for both stories.

Indeed, it is salutary how often companies with obstructive press offices end up as the subject of critical news stories. Another example in the UK has been Yorkshire Water, which has been derided for failing to maintain water supplies, for its charges, and on a host of lesser counts. Similarly, with Britain's large supermarket chains, notably Sainsbury, which considers most of its business out of the public domain. These same supermarkets are now being harried for allegedly excessive prices and profits. In the business information back-room, each one of these companies has been notorious for its closed-door policy to journalists.

## The aftershock

There are some companies that won't lock you into secrets, and don't lock you out. They rely instead on abuse and threats. Much of this is deeply mundane. The line-by-line analysis of a

> ### Shades of public access
>
> If publication means going public, being posted on the internet means inviting the world in. That makes people nervous, even more nervous than when they are talking to reporters. The financial disclosure statements of America's leading judges are officially public records. Details were given to the *Wall Street Journal*, and even the *Kansas City Star* – but not to APBnews.com, which, in December 1999, filed a public access action against US authorities in an effort to obtain the information. For the judges, total disclosure on the internet was a step too far. From where they were sitting the new media looked not just public, but far too accessible.

story by an aggrieved press officer amounts to little more than a time-consuming chore for reporters, as they pull out analysts' notes, industry comparators and the company's own annual report to support every point made in a news story. That said, such conversations can become extremely unpleasant and personal. Sometimes they don't come from the press office either, but from senior executives. Best-known for this was the British retail chain Marks & Spencer.

Marks & Spencer used to be viewed as a strikingly efficient and well-run company. But the very culture that produced its formidable internal efficiency, and the closest of relationships with its suppliers, was the same culture that alienated journalists and analysts, and eventually undermined its own business performance. Marks & Spencer believed firmly in being in control. It would brook no failure in meeting its needs, and it expected everyone involved in its operations to meet its specifications. If it believed the chief executive of a leading supplier was failing, it acted to remedy the situation. Similarly, it set out to control the news.

The group's press office was a standard gate-keeping operation: a role it performed more deftly than in Shell's case, with calls returned and refusals

## The self-censorship balance

Is the concentration of the media into conglomerates increasing self-censorship and editorial interference?

**No**. Pressure from advertisers is less threatening to a large and diversified business. The same is true of political pressure brought to bear on editors. A more powerful media is a freer media.

**Yes**. The problem is not size, but motives. Media conglomerates are in business to make profits. Legal actions and withdrawn advertising are expensive.

**Definitely yes**. Writing about your own group's other businesses is sticky – the 1998 decision by Disney-owned ABC news to kill a story about the inadequate security checks on staff at Disney World, Florida.

polite. But M&S did not stop at a tight lid. It was also unusually aggressive in policing the media.

There are in any country a handful of powerful businessmen who will think nothing of complaining to an editor or senior management about the work of a particular journalist or analyst in an effort to control news content. I have never known of a case where this has cost a reporter his job – it can damage careers, but it can equally add to a journalist's in-house credibility. However, there are many analysts who have been invited to quit after complaints by a powerful client about the negative nature of their comments.

In Marks & Spencer's case, complaints, whilst pursued with great alacrity and hostility, were normally made directly to the reporter concerned. Journalists were often stormed at, abused or derided. This kind of treatment might be viewed as a necessary evil of life as a journalist. But it is surprising how little it happens. Moreover, anyone who would diminish its efficacy should try receiving a similar roasting in his or her own professional life, and see if it doesn't achieve a 'steer-clear' outcome. Marks & Spencer was also litigious. Journalists who produced stories that were critical of the group faced the distinct likelihood that they would end up having to defend them in court, another daunting prospect.

Taken together, this combination of closed doors and aggressive pursuit was very effective in deterring journalists, and certainly prolonged M&S's days as a company above reproach. But it, similarly, left a trail of pent-up bad will and distrust, which finally manifested itself in two sets of stories. The media gave Sir Richard Greenbury a very rough ride when he acted as chairman of the first committee on corporate governance, ridiculing his tactics and attacking his methods. Several years later, journalists were only too happy to provide extensive coverage on the group's retailing difficulties, and promote debate on its senior management structure – again the butt was Sir Richard personally. Less controversial figures could have expected a more sympathetic press in similar circumstances.

Still, gratifying as it would be to say that bullying the press doesn't work, it clearly does, for a time. Perhaps one of the most extreme examples of litigious bullying was that of publishing tycoon Robert Maxwell, whose empire remained beyond the scope of even the bravest of journalists, until the door was opened by the peculiar manner of his death.

However, there are ways forward. If you are dealing with a company that will go after you if you write anything other than glowing sales copy, get your support in place first. Make sure senior management understands the situation, and let senior editors determine the level of pressure the publication is willing to sustain.

At the *Financial Times* (*FT*), when complaints are made to the editor, reporters are required to substantiate each point raised. The outcome is determined by the quality of the reporting, not by the bitterness or volume of the complaint. The same cannot be said of the more insidious requests for breakfast or lunch or dinner with the editor, aimed at providing a forum for non-specific complaints about one or several journalists. But even then, where companies are seeking to bully, their complaints are likely to backfire. The apocryphal tale at the *FT* is of the senior executive who collared the editor at a dinner for a lengthy and pompous complaint about the bias of his publication and the calibre of his journalists, only to deliver the entire litany with his flies undone! Such harassment earns the respect of no one within the media; and respect is something companies need if they are to succeed.

For you, it is important to hang on to the knowledge that almost all business writers come up against this type of nonsense. Grin, bear it, and work harder at exposing the truth (because if a company is run by bullies, it's not just journalists who get a hard time).

# ▶ The freebies

Any laboratory monkey will tell you that control is not all electric shocks and no food. Long before companies bully journalists, they court them. Lunches are proffered and paid for. Trips are mooted and facilitated. Gifts are purchased and distributed. And hypocrisy gets writ large. The official line of almost any news service you care to name is that journalists accept little from the companies they write about. The reality is that reporters who don't at some time accept some assistance of financial value, however small, are as rare as hens' teeth.

Perhaps the main reason is that much of this stroking is low-budget and distinctly helpful: lunches being the prime example. Breaking bread and establishing contact is as useful for writers as for companies. All that bonhomie and familiarity mean you get more information, and it makes it harder for contacts to later stonewall or lie to you. But it also makes it tougher to maintain your objectivity. Too many shared flagons of wine and you're not going to be running headlines exposing an executive's strategic cock-up.

The justification of establishing contacts can also see journalists cashing in on more glamorous corporate hospitality. In reality, you don't get much conversation with the management team while watching *La Traviata*, though you may occasionally get a titbit stoking up in a hospitality tent at Wimbledon. Mainly what you get is free opera and free tennis. The professional justification for accepting these invitations is pretty weak, and ironically, there are few gains for the company either, in terms of control. Writers are by temperament anti-establishment: you don't sign up for a lifetime of lifting the veil if you're quietly satisfied with the way things look with the veil down. Invites to lavish society extravaganzas can often serve to heighten a writer's sense of distance from those they write about.

The same is true of corporate gifts, from CD players to bottles of whisky. Viewed and treated as stash in the them-and-us game, many are pooled, to be auctioned or raffled back at the newsroom; some are swapped or passed on to colleagues, and others are just kept as the unlikely matching of need by coincidence. No one cares about them very much, and if any writer does end up distorting the truth with a gift in mind he's a rare exception.

## Companies' news agenda

- ◆ Sales are strong and rising.
- ◆ Prices are firm or rising.
- ◆ Product development is strong.
- ◆ All operations are safe and efficient.
- ◆ Employees are happy and appropriately rewarded.
- ◆ Management is acting in the best interests of shareholders.

Trips, however, really are a hard one. Facility trips are common in business journalism, and there are really compelling reasons why journalists participate. When a company opens its doors and puts itself on show you get to see things you would just not otherwise see. Moreover, for all that companies attempt to cover every crack, when they invite you into their own homes you learn things about them they don't even know about themselves. These are the reasons why we accept the three-day trips to a company's US sites, or the one-week tour of its subsidiaries in China. This is a chance for real insight. Indeed, because these operations are conducted on private property, it's usually the only way of getting a look.

The risk is that we get corrupted along the way. The smart hotels, grand meals and scheduled entertainments may have nothing to do with this. It's Stockholm Syndrome – the psychology of 24-hour contact and shared confinement. After two days on a coach with the management team, you're in danger of becoming a hostage turned terrorist.

> No one has made you sign away your right to use your eyes, ears and brain as an independent.

That's supposing you felt like 'the other side' to begin with. There are some who seem to swallow the line being fed through trips without a question-mark. Don't do it. Accepting an all-expenses paid is about applying your skills as a business assessor and writer to this particular company/ industry/ region. It may have put itself to the top of your pile by facilitating the examination, but that's all. No one has made you sign away your right to use your eyes, ears and brain as an independent.

In short, the real crunch with freebies is whether they pass the Private Eye test – named after the UK's eponymous satirical magazine. Before you accept, just ask yourself: 'Would I be embarrassed (or worse?) if details of this trip/gift/hospitality were made public?'.

## ▶ Spotting the holes

For all the bluster, juggling and attempts to befriend, those who try to control us are rarely doing more than pushing a close to transparent agenda (see box opposite).

A surer way of doing this is to achieve the business that lives up to the claims. If it's true, companies don't need to control us to see it written. Happily, there's a growing camp of companies that's twigged this. Control is of itself a bad sign – so they don't do it.

This has delivered the occasional delight of a company that answers all requests for information promptly and fully. But it hasn't yet produced the press release that gives all sides of a case, although some companies have tried. Monsanto, in an advertising campaign of desperate tone designed to head off controversy about genetically modified food, even advertised contact details for contrary points of view.

Generally, even where a company is giving all the information it has, it still won't be speaking for, or perhaps even aware of, the losers. In games theory it is possible for an event to produce only winners. Similarly, in business there are situations from which everyone benefits, but they are exceedingly rare. The norm is that there are winners and losers.

There is no reason and no need for companies to give all sides of this picture – this is your job. You need to spot the missing information by identifying the other people who will be affected by an event: the possible range isn't likely to go beyond shareholders, employees, customers, competitors, suppliers and neighbours.

You also need to be clear on the company's news agenda, as mentioned. By understanding that this is the picture the company is trying to paint with the facts it has, you will find it easier to spot the holes, and, more importantly, the extremely careful wording. Moreover, the importance of understanding agendas goes beyond recognizing where distortions are liable to occur. Many announcements are made because publicity, of itself, will make a difference to the outcome.

Such announcements often make good stories. But you do need to be clear about the reasons why this information is being put to you. This may be clearly explained, for instance with an announcement from a pressure group. But what about a spokesman who is suddenly willing to divulge all sorts of details during a takeover

### Why my good news is your bad news

- A port authority's perspective on port fees will not be the same as a shipping line's.

- A company may see a new product's utility, where a scientist sees its environmental cost .

- A company's reference to productivity may equate to a trade union's reference to job cuts.

- A stumble by one company may add up to a sales boom for its competitors.

battle? This happens frequently, and almost always because publicity will strengthen the negotiating hand of the source supplying the information.

No organization ever puts out a press release, or makes an announcement, without reason. Normally announcements are either required by law or intended to promote an organization's image with investors and customers. Where information is sent, or volunteered, to a journalist and it falls outside these broad categories, never make the mistake of overlooking the motive of the supplier. Companies that deliberately use the press are far more informative than the closed-door brigade, and are often good news for journalists: but their information is biased, with intent. It is only by understanding the agenda behind the announcement that journalists can unravel the bias, and do readers the service of delivering the information AND the agenda.

> **No organization ever puts out a press release, or makes an announcement, without reason.**

## ▶ Playing judge and jury

Covering all angles is the essence of balance. But that's not the same thing as putting every side in equal measure, without discernment. Of course, you can stay out of a lot of trouble, and spare a great deal of effort, if you write about everything with equal weight, no comparisons, and no information about strengths and weaknesses. For every comparison there is an aggrieved party: this is dangerous territory.

But what of the reader? Comparatives are essential to useful business information: which is the cheapest, which is growing the fastest, which is performing best or worst and why? So too is information about flaws, bonuses and booby traps. This places any business writer in the middle of a minefield.

Quite apart from hurting the feelings of senior company executives, they face the problem of ensuring accuracy, often at speed. A large amount of the information that they come across is sensitive. Much of it is not trustworthy. And they do have to convey judgements. There is a myth of journalism that the best of news coverage is factual and non-judgemental, and the best of journalists make no judgements, relaying the facts as they exist. But it is a myth. You are making judgements from the moment you sift through a pile of potential leads, or hover at the wings of a conference

**Comparatives are essential to useful business information.**

quizzing people who know. You decide what to leave out, and what to put in. You decide what information can be trusted, and above all you decide what news angle to pursue: nearly every business news story is built around a single point or thread, as identified by either the reporter or the news editor.

In balancing the arguments around this thread, you need to understand the way in which contrary views reflect different priorities, different views of the world and different motives.

Only then can you filter out, turn down or explain views that amount to deliberate and systematic distortion. Take the private comments of one chairman of a German conglomerate, when questioned about the mismatch between his company's outlook for its markets and the comments of many others in the sector: 'If we suggest that prices are likely to fall, our customers immediately come to us demanding price cuts, and prices do fall. We have to be optimistic.'

Sound as this reasoning is, no company can defy gravity. Corporate expectations are not the only determinant of prices. Where companies believe that their views move markets, writers cannot present this information as a reflection of prevailing market conditions. The same is true in many areas of business coverage. If a public company is experiencing difficulties, the last thing it wants to do is to cap it all by triggering a share price slump on the back of its own comments about its performance. It will have statutory obligations to notify shareholders of problems, but companies will often delay such announcements for as long as they can in the hope that the problem can be resolved without alerting outsiders. In short, companies are almost bound to minimize their difficulties in public, just as any of us would.

Of course, over the long term, you get to learn who distorts. Since all companies experience difficulties of one kind or another, and all prices move, it does eventually become clear which companies – and which executives – can be trusted to give an honest commentary. Thus history and background, or the ability to glean both through research, help the writer in identifying bias. But the ground is never safe. Even a highly trusted contact may lie when the stakes are high enough. Then your judgement delivers a story that's worse than unbalanced: it's wrong, which is why well-judged writing uses supporting evidence. In Chapter 11 we look at ways of testing assertions by gathering data that reveals the importance and even truth of the claims that are made to us. Do this and you won't go far wrong on the balance score. The only remaining pitfall will be your own agenda as a journalist.

## Your own agenda

Freedom of information is held up as one of the necessary checks and balances in a democratic society, precisely because there is a role for the journalist as a watchdog. But this role can itself create monsters, as journalists hunt for exposés that do not exist, or criticize unjustly. The journalists-as-scorpions camp would say that most journalists do this, nearly always. But this is a confusion of the nature of news and the nature of journalists. News has to be partial. People do not want 100 per cent of the information:

> The mission to expose weakness is supposed to be part and parcel of producing a full and balanced summary.

they couldn't possibly absorb it, and nor could any news service provide it. News services must be selective, and for that reason they tend to concentrate on that which is new, or changing, or unusual. This distorts, because normal events and experiences are omitted.

However, journalists should always be on guard against losing sight of the upside. The mission to expose weakness is supposed to be part and parcel of producing a full and balanced summary. It is not meant to be the be-all and end-all of business news, although there is a marked tendency in that direction.

I once visited a company that was just about to spin out from a much larger group. It had long been the underdog, starved of funds and viewed with little respect by the rest of the group. Its employees were delighted to be going it alone. The place was rich with excitement, renewed resolve and creative solutions. Having visited many companies in the same sector, it seemed clear to me that this company was set to outperform its peers. It did. Even when the sector entered a recession, the company delivered well above average growth, profits and development. However, back at base, the positive slant of my news analysis triggered a degree of concern. It is very easy to get trapped into the notion that no bad news indicates shallow reporting. In fact, sometimes, things really are going rather well.

Considering most companies' efforts to get us to be unreservedly positive, it is not surprising that at every turn we are required to demonstrate we have not 'gone soft' in the face of this pressure. But it is possible to end up going too far the other way. I recall one environment correspondent who was determined not to be seen as sympathetic to environmentalist groups. The resulting copy was seriously unbalanced, departing from all norms of claim, counterclaim and supporting evidence. In fact, the environmentalists never got a look-in.

However, while this was an overreaction, the concern was a legitimate one. Where journalists have become too attached to their roles as watchdogs, they can lose sight of the agendas of others within society who perform a similar role. When an environmental group sends out a press release about water quality, or a shareholders' rights group comments on a company's actions, they do so with just as much vested interest in sympathetic coverage as does any company. There will, necessarily, be another point of view.

In sum, journalists who discover no areas of sensitivity, or weaknesses in a case, or reluctance to divulge, or alternative perspective are living on another planet, whatever their area of coverage. But those who end up criticizing everything are not demonstrating their depth and prowess as journalists. They are merely revealing that they lack the confidence to be discerning, no matter what the pressures around them.

## ▶ Insider trading

Beyond our own agendas, and weaknesses in judging situations, there is the biggest pit of all: dishonest gain. As a business journalist you are frequently going to be an insider on public information. You will get embargoed news announcements, given early so that you can prepare a news story ahead of time. You will get scoops, which until they've appeared on your news service, really are not in the public domain. And you will write many other stories that you know are going to affect a share price – and *you* know that many hours before anyone else does.

> **As a business journalist you are frequently going to be an insider on public information.**

This sets up a nasty little loophole for unfair gains on the stock market. In the UK, the USA, and many other countries, exploiting this information for personal gain is called insider trading, and it is classed as fraud. Insider trading is not just illegal, it's criminal. In truth, you face more temptation in this regard than almost anyone in business, because you can create the inside information. In Chapter 4 we looked at the way a mention in *Business Week* moved the prices of shares. A journalist only needs to say something's good, and it moves the price up, as people buy on that recommendation. If journalists buy shares and then recommend, they can turn a tidy profit on the sale – a trick known as price ramping. So serious are the concerns about journalists profiting from this kind of abuse that many news services insist on contracts limiting or prohibiting journalists from trading shares at all. Some even preclude share trading by the journalist's friends or family.

The bottom line is that insider trading and price ramping are the acts of crooks and thieves. And the law is clear. However, the insider trading rules will affect you as a journalist, even if you do not turn into a crook, because they also apply to companies. Companies can fall the wrong side of these laws not just by misusing inside information, but by equipping others to do so. This means that in two very specific situations, companies are going to be extremely careful about talking to you. These two special cases are during an initial public offering (IPO) of shares – that is, in the immediate run-up to a company going public – and ahead of the announcement of financial results.

At these times, companies are not allowed to say anything to you as a reporter that might move the share price. In other circumstances, this would be simple. As soon as companies know something that could affect their share price they are obliged to announce it to the stock exchange – and thus make it a matter of public record. Then they can talk to you about it. But IPOs and financial results follow a timetable, which means that things will be known by the inside parties ahead of the public announcements.

Nonetheless, the difficulties for companies in this are grossly exaggerated, partly by the legal profession in the USA, which demonstrates its worth to a company by suggesting that this area is a minefield, and partly by companies themselves, as a shield behind which to hide awkward information.

In reality, even during an IPO and ahead of financial results, share-price sensitive information should by law be communicated to actual or potential shareholders. As long as companies are observing these rules, they will encounter few problems through indiscreet comments to journalists.

Nonetheless, you will often encounter closed doors, with insider trading rules held up as the reason. Typical, in the UK, is the institution of 'closed season'. Many companies observe a kind of short-term purdah, refusing to speak to anyone from the business press in the run-up to their financial results. In extreme cases, this can see companies close down their public communication for two months out of three. This is quite voluntary on their part. It is not required by the London Stock Exchange rules. And it is clearly unethical, insofar as the rules state absolutely that shareholders should be kept fully informed: an outcome that sits awkwardly with an information 'closed season'.

In the USA, where freedom of information is enshrined in the constitution, this kind of practice is rarely seen.

For you as a journalist, be clear, whenever a company refuses to talk to you, it's a custom not a requirement, and one that is left over from a bygone era, when shareholders were poorly served by the companies they owned *and* by the law.

‘Where is the knowledge we have lost in information?’

T.S. Eliot

# 7

# Effective research

## ▶ No facts, no story

Managers are not the only ones suffering from data overload. Journalists are inundated with information. Press releases, wires, specialist publications, research findings and management consultancy reports: all flood in.

> Managers are not the only ones suffering from data overload. Journalists are inundated with information.

But the match between this mass of incoming material and the information you need to do your job is slender. Almost every story requires additional research, and most will be dominated by content you have had to hunt out. It is this information which is the value of your news service. The top line from a press release will be relayed by many. The event reported by the wires can, similarly, be tracked down by anyone with ease. But when you build that top line into a news story that explains and interprets, you deliver a working tool.

In short, your research skills will dictate the quality of your stories to a greater degree than any other element. It doesn't matter if you write like a dream – if you haven't found the facts that explain why and how this story matters, the reader will be left with a confection, not a guide. However, research eats up the hours. Nor is there any link between the time thrown at it and the results yielded. Blind alleys are plentiful. Which is why, in this chapter, we look at ways of making your research really effective. These are the tips and short-cuts that allow journalists to create a solid news analysis, from nothing, in just a few hours, and news stories that make sense in less time still.

# ▶ Research from scratch

As long as you are writing about business, there will be stories you have to research from scratch. There will not be a contact in your book, or a file in your office, that even touches on the subject. Yet no one is going to award you extra time because you are starting empty-handed. You just *have* to learn how to find the facts quickly, no matter what the topic.

> **Effective research requires that you know what you are looking for and where to go to get it.**

So start with the cuttings. These are previous media articles on the same or similar subjects. Effective research requires that you know what you are looking for and where to go to get it. The cuttings should give you a starting point for both, which is well worth the 20 minutes to an hour that collecting and reading them will take. With the right person on the end of the phone, and the right questions in your mind, research becomes extremely rapid. By-pass the cuttings and you may still be scurrying around for information hours later.

Your own library may run a cuttings service. If it doesn't most online news services have searchable archives, which can be used in the same way as a cutting service. The most comprehensive of these is the adapted Profile database service available at ft.com, which draws on hundreds of media sources, many with regional or industry specialization. You may need to augment this search with cuts from the archive of a local, or particularly topical, news service.

> **Most online news services have searchable archives.**

Bear in mind, however, that some archives charge for cuttings, while others don't. Get to know which are free, and, if necessary, register with them. In time, most will be free of charge – consumers have shown remarkably little willingness to pay for archive material, and services that charge are increasingly abandoning fees in order to draw traffic that will attract advertisers.

Also beware of the search engine that sends you into a web search, rather than the news service's own archives. To begin with you want press copy. Why? Because journalists summarize. You don't want every last detail in vast quantities and with no sense of priority, which is what you will get from the web with a simple keyword search.

You want cuttings to give you an opening picture. Other journalists may well have been looking at a different aspect of the subject, the cuttings may be elderly – things have changed since – and may also contain mistakes. But, they are likely to do two things. First, they will highlight past preoccupations, and key issues. Second they are likely to quote expert sources – the relevant trade body, an analyst who's up to speed on this one, a business manager, or an academic. With this name you have your way in. Not that you will necessarily cite the same person. The point is that once you can speak to someone who knows about this subject, they will know other people who do too, and they can point you forward.

> **Research is a game of chance with rapidly diminishing returns. The further you have to go down a particular path, the *less* likely it is to yield anything.**

Sometimes, however, there just won't be cuttings. Whatever you do don't search too many archives. If you find nothing in a comprehensive media database and the most likely specialist publication, there is no point looking further. You may only have invested 10 minutes, but if you've got nothing at this stage you could continue for days and still get nothing. Look at it this way: if the most likely specialist source and the 3000 sources covered by something such as the FT archive have delivered not a word, what are your chances of getting more from less relevant sources or another 3000 individual searches?

Research is a game of chance with rapidly diminishing returns. The further you have to go down a particular path, the *less* likely it is to yield anything. So, always be prepared to change course, and do it quickly. This is a must.

## Searching the web

Your next best starting point is a web search. But don't use a search engine, unless you have a very good reason (one such would be using voila.fr for something French. Language is still a barrier on the internet, and most French material won't make it onto American or global search engines). Go straight to a meta-search engine. These run the same search through a bundle of engines. Everyone has their favourites (I like metacrawler.com). Some sift for duplicates. Others sort by relevancy. Some are built for speed, others for depth. The reason for going for a meta-search is that any one

## The Boolean search

◆ If you run a series of words with AND, written in capitals, in between each word (or +), the search will deliver documents that contain all the given words.

◆ If you run a series of words with OR between each word, it will deliver documents containing any one of the words listed.

◆ If you specify AND NOT it will exclude documents containing the word that follows.

search engine is merely a piece in the patchwork that is the internet. A search engine will be drawing material into its sights every minute of every day, but none have yet found a way of getting the lot. So spread your vision, without increasing your time searching, by covering several engines at once.

A greater problem with web searching, however, is not the material you can't access, but the volume of the material you can. You don't want 6533 results. You want 30, or better still ten, that are bang-on relevant. Achieving this depends on the way you construct your search query. It is better to define it too tightly and go back to look for more, than to spread your net too wide and end up with a mass of irrelevant material.

So, first be sure how the engine you're using works. Most (but not all) use a Boolean search (see box above). You may also get offered the option of an intelligent default, which will search for material that the software believes is related to your keywords (without containing them). I have never found this helpful in homing in on a specific subject – it just bumps up the results to no good end.

> A greater problem with web searching, is not the material you can't access, but the volume of the material you can.

For **general subject searches**, the tightest way to define a search is to go for an AND search, with several keywords. You need the obvious key phrase and then further words to narrow things down. This requires a little imagination, but you'll find it becomes second nature very quickly. For a search about the Japanese plastics industry add to this key phrase consolidation (people only write consolidation when they are giving a broad sweep of the state of the industry). Similarly, for a search about the state of the world bond market you need to add words that will eliminate daily bond market reports, or brokers' services, except where they are giving the big picture – possibles might be total, annual, or year-end. Or for a search on the children's book market, you will want to exclude online shops and book reviews, so you could add trend, publishing business, or global sales. Any of these should do the trick. If you still get too many results, run a new search with *more* key words.

When you're researching **a specific company**, it's also useful to track down its site. This should come near the top of any company name search, but you can also just go straight to the site. It will nearly always be the company name, followed by .com, for a large company, or the national tag for smaller companies – .de for Germany, .fr for France, .co.uk in the UK, and so on.

For **an individual**, try adding their job title and 'children'. The chances are that if you've got the name, the job title, and a mention of children, all in one place, you're looking at a profile – you could similarly try 'married', or 'hobbies'. And a profile is a good place to start, be it in briefing yourself ahead

## Listening in …

Usenet news groups cover a huge range of topics, putting you in an e-mail ring with others interested in the same thing. You can post queries (anyone know a source for …?) or just monitor the debates. Best of all, you can search a large proportion of the world's news group discussions by keyword, through the discussion search option at www.dejanews.com. It's a great way of getting offbeat material, or picking up on particular cases, although inevitably patchy. You can also sign up for listserv e-mail groups, which automatically share all e-mails posted with all members. These can be set up by anyone, anywhere, and are usually unadvertised and closed to outsiders. However, you can search some of the growing directories, and apply by e-mail if there's one you'd really like to be part of. Try catalog.com/vivian/interest-group-search.html or www.liszt.com or tile.net/lists.

of an interview, or for any piece relating principally to that person.

In all these cases, don't worry about over-defining a search. If the search comes back with nothing, widen it. By starting so tight, you increase your efficiency. If you get anything, it is likely to be what you need. If you don't, redefining the search takes a moment, whereas wading through irrelevant material can take many, many moments (hours).

When you do get something promising, watch the source. Anyone can post anything on the net. Don't confuse a 15-year-old's high school essay, with a Harvard PhD. When you have the starting point you're looking for, remember it is just that. You can follow a trail online, through a company's own site, or perhaps to a trade organization. But as soon as you've identified an expert, get off-line, and on the phone.

Researching online is a hit or miss affair, and very slow. It's a fantastic tool as first base, and it will certainly enable you to reach further, quicker. But once you've found what you're looking for, you need to talk to someone who you can probe for missing pieces, and quiz for explanations. It's much quicker.

Finally, if you've got the real ace assignment today – the one where there are no cuttings, and nothing useful (that you can find) on the internet – pick up a phone directory and think laterally. Do you know of any company involved in this field – call its press office. Which trade organization might know about this? Ask your colleagues. Ask a business or science library. Ask a museum. Just don't get stuck on any one path. If something doesn't work, change course. But keep going. Because rest assured, if it exists, you *will* be able to find out about it.

# ▶ Interviewing

Interviewing skills are so essential to strong coverage that we look at them in depth in Chapter 9. But here, for now, are a few pointers that could save you a great deal of time, and considerably increase the value of what you glean.

◆ Before you pick up the phone, jot down four or five keywords that will remind you of the main information you're looking for.

◆ Make sure you have the right person. Don't waste time quizzing someone who doesn't know. You have to distinguish 'don't know' from 'won't say' to know whether persistence and guile might pay. But never waste time with someone who wants to help, but can't. Get passed on.

◆ Get things explained. I remember one *FT* trainee driving his colleagues nearly mad with the basic questions he was asking in his interviews. But he was an extraordinarily good journalist. You can't please everyone all the time and your first loyalty is to your readers. Your explanation can't be clear unless you understand the ramifications yourself. And it's better to look an idiot in the interview than in the paper. So don't let a point past your ears that your brain isn't happy with. Stop. Ask. And then move on. EXCEPT where the flow really matters. If your interviewee is happily heading into deep water, and a brake might remind them that they are, after all, talking to a journalist, jot down a keyword, and come back for comprehension later.

◆ Get supporting material sent. Also ask who else is good on the subject. You may still have a must-fill gap left in your story at the end of this phone call.

This will probably be the end of the line in a starting-from-scratch story. You should have gleaned some kind of framework and a few useful details from cuttings and the internet. You should have filled that out with pertinent and current information from those in the know – in one or in ten interviews (you can rarely say which it will take). But the process doesn't end there: the best coverage comes not from rapid research, but from cumulative research.

## Contacts

Great contacts spell great business news, and you are going to need the full set: observers, experts, insiders, and decision-makers. You cannot, however, create working relationships with everyone in a day. Even if you inherit a contacts list, it will be a list of contact details, not of contacts. You won't know who is good on what, who is more open, or more lateral. Moreover, few people talk as freely to someone they don't know. And *your* best sources will be the people with whom you have the most natural rapport: which is something you really cannot glean from your predecessor's list, however well annotated it is.

**Great contacts spell great business news.**

So, your own contacts list needs to be built, one step at a time, and the place to begin is with the **corporate press office**. The press officer, or external corporate PR, is your gateway to a company. Occasionally a press officer will pull out all the stops to assist you even though you are a total stranger. But as a rule the better he or she knows you the better will be the volume and quality of information on offer. On any business beat, setting up meetings with the press officers of key companies, often in the office *and* over lunch, is one of your first tasks. They will normally give you a fairly detailed rundown of the company. You also need to get the annual reports, and any and all briefings for your files. You need to agree the ground rules

## Spreading our bets for us

A range of analysts' pre-tax profit forecasts in June 2000 for the full year, and their recommendations.

| Pearson | | Unilever | | ICI | |
|---|---|---|---|---|---|
| BUY | 433 | UND | 2775 | BUY | 404 |
| ADD | 421 | HOLD | 2939 | UND | 487 |
| ADD– | 480 | HOLD | 3271 | SELL | 506 |
| BUY | 499 | ADD | 2979 | BUY | 464 |
| BUY+ | 471 | OUT | 2320 | HOLD | 433 |
| OUT | 410 | ADD | 3245 | HOLD | 447 |
| BUY | 462 | BUY | 3200 | S/HOLD | 475 |
| ADD | 426 | ADD+ | 3200 | BUY | 475 |
| ADD | 405 | BUY | 3182 | HOLD | 469 |
| | | BUY | 2674 | NEUT | 445 |
| | | BUY | 2330 | | |

OUT = outperformer
UND = underperformer
S/HOLD = sell/hold
NEUT = neutral.

for how you are going to work together, and you need to give a good feel for your areas of interest. In fact, this particular working relationship is so crucial to your success as a business journalist that it is covered in much more detail in Chapters 6 and 8.

> The greater the depth of an analyst's research and knowledge, the less will be his tendency to adopt groundless postures.

Your next stop should be the **stockbrokers' analyst**. Analysts will often have collected the information you seek, have the contact details for the executives you want to talk to, and know the places to find both. Often referred to as sell-side analysts, their job is to service stock-brokers' clients with investment advice (see box). They talk to everyone, from huge institutional investors to private individuals. They normally specialize by industry, covering a sector, such as telecoms, defence or biotechnology. However, some have regional specialisms, covering perhaps Belgian stocks, or Chinese companies listed in Hong Kong.

There *is* a catch. Normally, sell-side analysts are rewarded with cash bonuses, often as large as their basic salaries, for the amount of share trading they generate in their sector. This mission to generate trade is both an attraction and a peril in terms of their usefulness as a source. On the plus side it means analysts are constantly looking for new angles, or clues to the future. The minus is the way in which forecasts and recommendations vary dramatically between brokers' houses, and over time. Generating trade means having something new to say – perhaps even when there is nothing new to say. This can make for some off-the-wall analysis! You also cannot expect an analyst to say anything objective about a stock that his house manages, or is advising on the corporate finance side. That said, when it comes to working out who you

> **Estimates we love to have**
>
> Analysts will often have estimated:
> - sales and profits for businesses not broken out in the accounts of a conglomerate;
> - the impact of an external change – such as how much of a company's business is conducted in the Mexican peso, or how exposed it is in Indonesia or in the USA, or to a 1 per cent rise in interest rates;
> - ratios between the current share price and a company's future earnings as forecast by the analyst (prospective price/earnings ratios).
>
> See Chapter 10 on how to use these numbers

can trust, the ground rules are not complex: the greater the depth of an analyst's research and knowledge, the less will be his tendency to adopt groundless postures. So be prepared to quiz the logic, and supporting evidence, mercilessly.

When you have worked out who's worth talking to, here's what you can hope to get:

- forecasts for a company's future sales and profits, with reasoning attached, and plenty of other estimates, for context (see box above);

- analysts' notes, detailing a company's activities, its strengths and weaknesses, industrial issues that are forcing change and upcoming strategic issues;

- analysts' briefings. Companies will often give analysts detailed presentations on businesses that they refuse to give to business news writers. In my experience, analysts have always been happy to pass on these presentations, in full: the hard copy, numbers, charts and even the questions and answers;

- industrial context, such as details of main competitors, a company's market share, how fast a particular market is growing, the prevailing

---

## Gossip, gossip and more gossip

**Fund managers**. Analysts spend a lot of time talking to fund managers. They usually know what is driving funds' buying and selling, and, better still, where spats are looming between large shareholders and company executives.

**Executives**. Analysts also spend a fair amount of time with company executives: on trips, at conferences, and on-site. They can often inject the colour that fills out the public face of a chief executive, or other directors.

**Bankers**. Analysts are also on the edges of the investment banking grapevine, and while they are unlikely to gossip about the activities of their own colleagues, you can expect them to be avid collectors of details on what other banking teams are up to.

---

prices for raw materials and final products, and upcoming regulatory issues;

◆ share-trading summaries, giving a thumbnail sketch of who's buying and selling a company's shares and why;

◆ other sources, pointers to individuals in-the-know, and places to get data;

◆ tip-offs. Analysts will never be your main source of tip-offs, but you can expect a steady trickle, be it a call to say the competition authorities have dawn-raided, or a mention in passing that fund managers are after the hide of a particular chief executive;

◆ gossip – see above.

If this all sounds like such a beanfeast you can never imagine the need to talk to anyone else, beware. Analysts place a much greater emphasis on numbers, spreadsheets, and micro-detail than you are ever going to. It's fabulous to have this expertise to turn to, but it may take you little further in your search for the big picture, evidence of a trend, or even in just finding your story. Moreover, analysts are always a secondary source. These observers are not insiders, they just spend a lot of time quizzing the insiders.

In sum, I have seen analysts both overrated and underrated as a source. I recall working for one news editor who considered a news story inadequate for publication if its perspective on a company's prospects had not been checked with three analysts. At the other end of the scale, another news editor considered news stories sourced to analysts as the equivalent of coming up with a story line while musing in the shower. It was her view that an analyst was worse than a second-rate source: an analyst was no source at all.

Well, they can't both be right. The truth is that analysts work, year in, year out, with a smaller range of companies and a more tightly defined subject area than almost any business news writer. As the suppliers of an external and well-informed snapshot of a company they are unsurpassed. Many of them will know companies' senior executive teams personally, meet them regularly, and spend enormous amounts of their working time seeking out detailed background information about companies' opera-

## Collude with care

Passing on information that moves a share price can end your career, and even lead to a criminal conviction, so avoid:

1 Leading questions. Every now and then the very fact that you are asking a question will flag up an issue – and an issue, at that, which is about to get press coverage. Try to get there sideways.

2 Relating obvious insider information. You will be talking to many other contacts, and will certainly end up with information the analyst does not have. Before referring to any of it, be sure it is not share price sensitive prior to, or in the absence of, publication.

See Chapter 6, on insider trading

tions. In short, the best of them are as accurate a source on the state of a company's health or prospects as you are likely to find anywhere – except in the company's own filing system.

**Every broker and bank has analysts. Most will be happy to talk to the press. Some even seek publicity, as a way of attracting future clients.**

So how do you find them? Every broker and bank has analysts. You only need to ring the switchboard and ask for the research analysts. Most will be happy to talk to the press. Some even seek publicity, as a way of attracting future clients. However, others are bound by company policies forbidding them from talking to us. In fact, this kind of official policy is normally bypassed at an individual level, once trust and familiarity are established. This is partly because you are all interested in the same thing, which makes contact interesting, but, more than that, information never flows in one direction alone (see box above).

The dynamics are quite different when it comes to talking to **executives**. They want good publicity. This is such an over-riding consideration it will render 95 or even 99 per cent of what they say to you unuseable. They will hedge, fence, eulogize, dish out sound-bites and advertise. What they won't do is just talk about what's really happening. You will still be talking to them all the time. You will still use quotes. And, in time, a small number of executives will become 'contacts'. You'll probably take to these individuals immediately. They will talk to you candidly, be quite clear about what is on and off the record, and make themselves reachable at any time. It's unlikely you'll find one in ten who works this way. But the ones who do will contribute to your stories in countless ways, and across many subjects. The only problem will be maintaining the balance of your coverage. No matter how hard-nosed you are, when a company's top management is open, helpful and personable, it becomes counter-intuitive to highlight their weaknesses. As ever, you are the reader's servant – you want direct access, but you do have to find a way of running these relationships that respects the need for you to write down, as well as up.

In this regard, there are other sources within companies that will leave you with a freer hand. On smaller matters, and in particular areas of a business, the right people to have on your contacts list are the **business managers**. At a day-to-day level, they run the business, and know it inside out. They generally worry far less about the politics of talking to the writers of business news, and are more interested in relaying experiences as they really are. You can track them down through company switchboards, internal newsletters or, best of all, at specialist conferences. You will meet them on site visits, at industry-related dinners, and, sometimes they will just call you out of the blue. I've often been asked about tips, and where they come from. In fact, you will get more 'scoops' from these sources than from anyone else, but most business managers won't even look upon these inside pointers as tipping you off. Your news is their reality.

So far, these are all run-of-the-mill contacts. You would not expect to be covering any beat at all without talking to corporate press officers, sell-side analysts, executives and business managers. There are, however, other types of contacts that are really worth having – if you can get them. Good contacts within the **authorities** that oversee the companies you write about, notably the stock exchange and the competition authorities, are invaluable. These bodies gather a great deal of information about the companies they police. Much of it is technically public, but not published. When it does get

## The man from the intranet

There is only one reason for you to carry out research: to save the research time of managers. We looked in Chapter 3 at the information managers want in order to make better decisions: here are some thoughts for you on how to get it to them.

**Competitors**: set up competitor directories, with each company page offering links to a company's own website, to the relevant research notes from stockbrokers' analysts, and to incidental material relating to the operations of that competitor.

**Markets**: again, set up a reference, organized by type of market, with links to specialist sources. Get consultants' reports, and repackage them into online briefing notes that contain only the information that's germane to your managers.

With trade publications, do a weekly news alert, giving a two-line contents summary and page number for the three or four pieces that are really relevant to your audience and for anything else that might be of coincidental interest. *Think of the time saved when 30 managers just go straight to pages 3 and 8, and can skip the rest safe in the knowledge there's nothing in there for them.*

Similarly, across competitors, markets and technology, start thinking in terms of putting together your own briefing notes on topics really critical to your company. And make the notes of others available to all, in a database structure that makes them findable!

published, for example in a Monopolies and Mergers Commission study, there will be so much depth and insight, the result will be the best snapshot of an industry you are likely to see for the next several years. Then there is the information they have that is not for public consumption: often authorities will use this data to make sure you're not going up a blind alley, without actually revealing the numbers or reasons. In short, it will help you a great deal, in all your most controversial stories, if you are well-plugged in with the policemen (all of whom have press offices).

**Non-executive directors** are frequently overlooked as a source. They shouldn't be. These board members know a lot about the companies they help run and they often have an inclination towards independence. Indeed, the whole point of their status is that they are expert outsiders. You will regularly find them to be the most reliable, and most forthcoming of the knowledgeable sources, on a company's big issues. Of course they vary by temperament, but for steering you off a duff story, or discreetly proffering the company's view on an accurate, but unconfirmed angle, they really are a good bet.

There is also another, much more mysterious, type of analyst, known as the **buy-side analyst**. These are researchers and specialists who work for the huge investment funds, often pension funds. Some of these, fresh from college, rely for all their information on the sell-side analysts, offering very little real specialism, but rather an interface with the trading institutions. But other, more senior analysts, are spectacularly well-informed. An example would be a buy-side analyst who is responsible for the research into a company that his fund owns 9 per cent of: this guy is basically on the inside-track. But, he has very little interest in speaking to the media. These contacts are difficult to cultivate, but meaningful, offering extraordinary insights into the current issues for a company, as well as a strong feel for the preoccupations and trading strategies of the funds.

Another whole class of contacts are **corporate advisers**, most notably those with merchant banks. These will almost certainly be the most Machiavellian of your contacts. When it comes to efforts to make your news serve their ends, these advisers make the executives and external PR agencies look like amateurs. They will leak when a deal is tottering, or a predator is looming, and preserve stiff formality when there is nothing you can do for them. But for all that they are dangerously agenda ridden, and they are one of the most common ways of getting a rumoured corporate deal second-sourced. When you know already, they will often confirm. A few will even pass on great stories that are just great stories. For the rest, they offer grapevine value, in that they move in the world of corporate finance. They will usually know when companies are touring the banks with a new need. They will often know what other teams are up to, and they may sometimes be irked to have lost a deal to another bank. As a rule, business news is anathema to them, but work at it. Journalists plugged into the merchant banks get big scoops, regularly.

Finally, there are the fellow travellers. Other **business writers**, competitors though they may be, are also your colleagues. There will be many occasions when you work together to get the story. There will also be times when you turn to them for possible leads or contacts, explanation, context or historical background. You will also find that it makes sense to receive the publications they produce. In large part these will serve the same purpose, on an ongoing basis, as a cuttings search. But you will also come across things that are of interest to you from a different angle, or stories that you may wish to pursue further.

Similarly, you will often talk to **consultants**. Anyone can call themselves a consultant. It doesn't mean a great deal. The kinds that make sense on your contacts list are the industrial specialists, and, to a much lesser extent, management consultants. The industrial specialists will often compile statistics that are unavailable elsewhere. They may also have an unusual depth of knowledge and a close eye on new trends. The best tend to work within smaller consultancies. Larger organizations become increasingly preoccupied with the current vogue in management theory, whatever their espoused specialism. The more theoretical they become though, the harder it is to make sense of them as a journalist. You'll get the odd story from an issue-specific team, or from large research reports. You'll also get an occasional shot at a detailed case study – this can make really good copy. But otherwise, the gap between the theory they sell and the information you seek is almost unbridgeable.

> Statistics are something you should store like a squirrel. The more you collect, the better your stories will be.

**Trade organizations** can also be useful, but they are variable. Some seem to operate in a near information vacuum, while others are a locus for sectoral information. It seems to be key individuals, rather than the nature of the industry that distinguishes the good from the bad. From the best you can get voluminous information about the impact of government policies, key issues for the sector and even offbeat industry statistics. They may also be able to proffer specialist contacts within member companies.

## ▶ Reference material

Statistics are something you should store like a squirrel: beg them, borrow them, even … OK, no incitement here. But as we shall see in Chapter 11, it is these numbers that will allow you to demonstrate the significance of the events you are reporting. They are extremely time-consuming to hunt down on the day. The more you collect, the better your stories will be. So, don't stop at national statistics. Ask analysts where they get theirs, and sign up for your own. Collect them from port authorities, chambers of commerce – particularly in continental Europe – employers' organizations, trade unions or anyone else who's gone to the trouble of putting them together. Similarly, collect directories, of companies, exporters, analysts, university researchers, and anything else: they're filled with potential contacts for that one story in 20 that no one can help with.

Finally, don't overlook the compilation that will give you the line that makes sense of it all. These are real goldmines for business writers. Typical are collected corporate histories, science dictionaries, guides and bibliographies.

Information is your metier. What comes out may be more than went in, because of the links you've made. But be sure. If you've too little of the right stuff going in, you haven't a chance of delivering real value to your readers.

**'Making the simple complicated is commonplace'**

Charles Mingus

# 8

# The press release

▶ The start of the news chain

When you want to be understood, really understood, as in 'I may be nearly unconscious, but I'm **allergic** to penicillin' kind of understood, you make clear statements. When you want to be listened to, you make sure what you say is interesting, that it captures attention.

Companies need to be understood. They don't make clear statements, and they don't make sure that what they say is interesting. They issue press releases. Most are works of art when it comes to shying away from the meaningful and obscuring reality, but a pure headache when it comes to extracting the news. This is bad news for you, because we need that news: we're all affected by events that happen inside, or are first witnessed by, companies. And it's bad news for the companies too.

> Companies need to be understood. They don't make clear statements, and they don't make sure that what they say is interesting. They issue press releases.

Companies usually speak because they believe the more they are heard, the better they will do. Shareholders will better understand the business, and perhaps prove more loyal. Customers will know more about what a company offers, and perhaps buy sooner when they have a problem to solve. Mileage will be made too in the jostling of rivals, the marketing of image and the creation of public acceptance. Even when companies are obliged to issue statements – from annual results to profit warnings – the ability to engender understanding can only aid their cause.

Yet few press release writers seem able to bridge the communication gap. They issue too many statements. Announcements that are not news-worthy should not be made: they clog up communication channels and can even kill the chances of future releases by flagging up to journalists that a press officer, or a company, has no news judgement. And when companies do have something that could make the news they often blow it. The key point may be buried in hyperbole, obscured by technical jargon, saved until page three or omitted altogether. Surprisingly often, no one is even available on the contact number to help clear up some of this confusion.

Nevertheless, the press release remains *the* most common way of relaying business news to the news messengers. As we shall see, a well-honed press release can push a marginal news story to the top of the pile, just as a badly written one can ensure it goes no further than the bin.

## ▶ The sins that kill communication

There are five markers of a bad press release: jargon, hyperbole, buried leads, no news and excessive length. Each of them is death to a news story. And they usually appear several at a time. Take the following extract from a **six-page**, 1,901-word press release. This is the most informative section. What would your story be?

27 May 1999

### PeopleSoft Delivers Advantage Lifecycle Solutions

Knowledge Tool, Rapid Results Implementation Approach and
Services Deliver Maximum Value Throughout
PeopleSoft Lifecycle

PeopleSoft today announced general availability of PeopleSoft Advantage, a framework of technology and customer services designed to provide maximum value of ownership throughout the PeopleSoft systems lifecycle, including planning, implementation, production, and enhancement. PeopleSoft Advantage features the Advantage ToolKit (ATK), a web-enabled knowledge management solution designed to guide customers through every phase of the lifecycle. In addition, the new services include PeopleSoft Express, a rapid-results implementation approach offering customers a menu of implementation routes. PeopleSoft also unveiled lifecycle service and support programs offering direct access to specialised knowledge and support.

'Our customers are requiring new ways to deal with technological complexity and change, as well as ways to mitigate risk,' said Jim Bozzini, senior vice president of worldwide services at PeopleSoft. 'PeopleSoft Advantage provides a range of new and innovative knowledge tools and service programs, enabling customers to get the most value out of their PeopleSoft implementations in the most effective way.'

**Advantage ToolKit**

Introduced in managed release in November of 1998, ATK is an intuitive, web-enabled knowledge management solution designed to help project teams to more effectively implement, maintain and upgrade PeopleSoft solutions. Responding to individual customers' needs, ATK guides project team members through a roles-based approach to leveraging business processes, procedures, models, templates, samples, and related resources for every phase of the lifecycle.

Before you make excuses for this horror, like it's a specialist subject: it isn't. Isn't that shocking? This product is aimed at a broad business audience. More importantly, this is a **press** release. PeopleSoft wants people like **us** to write stories about 'Advantage'.

So, what is the advantage? Technology is only worth a jot if it delivers some benefits. If we can't grasp the gain, we won't grab the technology. In this case, it's nearly impossible to work out what the product is, let alone its advantages. In a thicket of technical and conceptual jargon (what is 'maximum value of ownership' anyway?), even the basics are clumsy, unless there is something more to 'general availability' than that the software is on sale? The net effect is a blank.

There is nothing about software stories that makes this kind of inaccessibility necessary – especially where a release is covering a product launch. If a product is sellable, a story about it can be made sellable. For instance, by taking the approach of the following extract from a two-page, 684-word press release:

18 March 1999

# PhoneLink saves independent travel agents
# 76% of the cost to access airfare, hotel and car hire booking deals

### PhoneLink launches Tel-Me Travel Express to the independent travel agent market

PhoneLink plc today launches Tel-Me Travel Express. The software is a light version of Galileo* which enables independent travel agents to operate more competitively in the travel market by providing more choice and better service for its customers. For a quarter of the normal price, Tel-Me Travel Express allows both IATA and independent travel agents (non-IATA agents) to directly access over 500 schedule airlines for up-to-the-minute seat availability and facilitate ticketing.

Ian Sinderson, Head of Strategic Planning at PhoneLink plc commented: 'Independent travel agencies have in the past been at a complete disadvantage in the travel market. Previously, they have either had to pay approximately £5,000 per year to access a computer reservation system, or personally liaise with its IATA ticketing partner in order to book a ticket, which is then passed on to the customer. The first option proves to be an expensive drain on resources and the second inefficient and expensive in time. Tel-Me Travel Express provides the means to force a healthy redress to the marketplace.'

Now, for just £99 per month, the agent can allow up to ten users per site to have direct access to a database of over 500 schedule airlines as well as have access to over 30,000 hotels and numerous car hire booking deals, all from the PC. Tel-Me Travel Express is available immediately to the 17,000 independent travel agents in the UK.

This press release is not steeped in jargon. The language is clear and, better still, statements and supporting evidence are interwoven, making the sum more convincing and more illuminating. The writer has also understood the news agenda of the business media, even down to the story's merit resting on the TOTAL benefit the product might deliver. Which is why PhoneLink has spelt out the size of the audience *and* gone some way to quantifying benefits. This may not be the most exciting piece of software you have ever read about, but the press release does allow you to see the potential the story holds. Conversely, PeopleSoft has offered no clue to any possible news angle.

In fact, these two extremes are typical. Press releases either commit most of the five sins, or none of them. Few writers, who realize how important clarity is, go on to bury the news. This applies equally with announcements that go too far in building a story's importance. Writers of puff have a knack of losing sight of the facts that matter. Indeed, as soon as they start down the path of communicating nebulous benefits through positive associations they get into trouble: it makes for hyperbole that is neither convincing nor credible. Take this release from car-maker Renault:

By harnessing the brand's essential values, namely daring, innovation, warmth and friendliness, plus respect for the environment, Renault Sport has developed a new generation of cycle delivering a panoply of new sensations. A complete family of models stands ready to appear, taking the lead from the all-new 'Tangara' mountain bike, a triumph of pure technology. The entire range will be distributed via the Renault sales network, starting in September.

Backed by years of expertise crafted in the world of Formula 1 (6 Constructors' World Championship titles and 5 Drivers' World Championship titles), Renault Sport has been keen to diversify and to bring its technical skills to bear on one of the most popular leisure activities in the world. Confronted with a sporting activity in ever greater demand, as much for keeping fit as for getting places, or for breaking free of constraints that are so much part of our modern lives, Renault Sport has wanted to give cycle enthusiasts everywhere the very best that its engineers have to offer.

Enhance both the traction and the degree of control inherent in the mountain bike by incorporating a car's fully fledged suspension systems similar to a car's shock absorbers: that was the challenge taken on by the F1 teams at Renault Sport. Two years of research and fine tuning, carried out in tandem with dynamic, Formula 1 style electronic testing and measuring were needed to bring this revolutionary new mechanism to fruition, a unit that is every centimetre a world first.

This suspension system (No Resonance System), is adapted to suit the most sports-oriented of mountain bike styles. It combines the comfort of a full-suspension mountain bike with the performance of a rigid model, reacting to jolts and impact without any loss of power. The principle underpinning NRS is all to do with separating out the operation of the rear suspension and the energy generated from pedalling.

The indisputable pluses of this technological first are clearly stated: it delivers greater pleasure to the rider by injecting more comfort and precision whilst retaining the unique sensations associated with the mountain bike; it heightens performance on heavily indented terrain; but, at the same time, extends the life expectancy of the bike by reducing its vulnerability to jolt and impact. Two models in the mountain bike range boast NRS: the Tangara (cross-country) and the Vanoise (Freeride).

Although the bicycle has become a real source of pleasure for family and individuals alike, it signifies nowadays a new type of lifestyle, a clear, unambiguous acceptance of new sets of values … .

So it continues, for another seven paragraphs! The lesson for press release writers is when you have something good to say, just say it. In this case, that wouldn't have taken too much skill. All the puff about cycling needs to go – it is at best banal. Similarly with all the repetition (I count six references to this being a technological breakthrough in just these opening 5 ½ paragraphs – and most of them overblown, from 'every centimetre a world first' to 'this revolutionary new mechanism'). Once is enough: this is new, how and why.

The rest then needs to be structurally unravelled. The gains for the cyclist should be hit in one place ONLY. Similarly with the technology (and its Formula 1-ness). And, finally, there are the missing elements. The significance of bike-selling through car outlets needs to be drawn out, as does the significance of this company's entry into the bike market.

In fact, there are several small jewels later in this press release. Almost at the close Renault tells us that it is to offer finance packages for purchasers of these bikes as it does with its cars, that it plans to provide a car-type service manual with the bikes, and that the bikes will be serviced by its car mechanics. This is interesting stuff – it certainly amounts to a new way of selling bikes. As such, it should be at the top of the press release, along with the technology announcement. This story is actually rather strong in its technology, marketing, company *and* industry implications. Yet the last two get no mention at all. I would like to know how much Renault is putting into this new venture. And what's this all about at the level of strategy – this is a car company. Why the departure? If there are good reasons we want to hear them. Similarly, at the industrial level, a miniscule amount of context would go a long way. Is the world spending £1billion a year on bikes, and rising, or £1million, and falling: how big is this market that Renault is targeting (and we are being asked to write about)? As things stand, only the superstars of corporate communication offer this kind of context – yet it really makes the difference between a story that runs, and no story.

# The importance of the story

News value is the guiding light of an effective press release. Get writers interested in the story and they'll stick with you through a fair multitude of written sins. Which is why the news comes first, no matter how important you think the rest is. News, by and large, is driven by audiences.

People who will (or might) be directly affected by an event are normally interested in reading about it. You need to know who these people are and tell us the size of this audience and how it will be affected.

> Get writers interested in the story and they'll stick with you through a fair multitude of written sins.

But don't stop there. Any really strong story is going to appeal to a broader audience still as an indicator of the future. There may be lessons to be learnt, or it may flag up a change that could eventually affect many more people. So run a check (see box). It's the answers to these questions that will decide whether a story makes a brief or one of the day's headlines.

To clinch the interest in an event's broader relevance you need to communicate just how unusual an event is, so contrast it with the norm (see Chapter 11). Also, at every stage you need to be scaling things. A big change for a big audience is a bigger story than a small hiccup for a tiny group of people. Again, we look at scaling in Chapter 11.

### Reaching a broader audience

- Is this a precedent?
- Does it conflict with, or throw any new light on, conventional wisdom?
- Could it mark the beginning of a trend?
- Does it hold lessons for managers, or others?

---

### Getting it right

- Imagine no one has ever heard of your company or what it does.

- Home in on the thing that people are going to care about most.

- Make that your opening idea, and say why it matters, and to whom.

- Convince the journalists about this, with real, solid, factual comparative information.

- Use language that is clear.

- Test the end product for the questions it raises – then answer them.

- Cut anything that isn't necessary to your tale.

- Give a (meaningful) contact point for further information.

- And if you can't find an angle that's going to raise an eyebrow somewhere – don't write a press release.

---

In sum, identifying audiences is essential to effective communication. No interested readers = no story. More than that, the nature of your audience dictates what you lead on, what you include and to whom you send the announcement. The alternative is throwing announcements to the wind.

## Making it live

So, you've got a news angle and you've got a news audience. Now build a story (see box). Most press releases would turn out just fine if writers understood from the outset that their task was to tell a tale. They would then convey real life in a way that could be understood: which is the whole point. A press release can require more work than many other stories in gathering facts: there's greater need to get the significant in and leave the insignificant out. It also needs to start with a punchline.

The end point is nothing more complicated than a tale well-told. Think about a results announcement given this way. Framed as a story about the state of health of a company it leaves the reader with coherent impressions. Presented as a formal, stilted and jargonized statement it leaves behind a jumble of figures and more figures and not too many facts.

The other thing about story-telling is that you tell it differently depending on who's listening. You edit out the dreary or shocking, and build up the appealing, be it for your mate in the pub, your partner, or your boss. The same is necessary with announcements to the press. Once you know who your audience is, you've a pointer straight to the media that feed that audience. What are the images that interest them? You only need to look at their news content for answers.

The *Financial Times* always wants statistical context. *FT* journalists don't want to know that your company is investing in a boiler-pipe firm, unless you also tell them that it will make your company the largest boiler-pipe manufacturer in Poland, or that it will cut the cost of pipes to boiler manufacturers by 10 per cent, or that it will increase the worldwide capacity for making boiler-pipes by 3 per cent at a stroke. The critical image for this newspaper is a picture of where an event fits into the wider world of business.

Similarly, a local newspaper wants the human angle. The more you personalize a story pitched at neighbours the better will be the take-up. An announcement that the town's water mains are to be upgraded will do far better if you give the names of those responsible for the scheme, as well as information about traffic delays, supply interruptions, and, perhaps, the news that those annual summer consumption restrictions are coming to an end. Then it becomes part of the town's upcoming experience, and not just a utility announcement. (See box above.)

## The Cluetrain Manifesto

Before the internet, people didn't hear much from companies. Corporate words got filtered through journalists. Now, anyone can go straight to the source, and many aren't very taken with the style.

Cluetrain is just one of the internet campaigns calling on companies to rediscover their lost humanity.

Says Cluetrain, in its manifesto (at www.cluetrain.com):

**Conversations among human beings *sound* human. They are conducted in a human voice.**

**Whether delivering information, opinions, poropoctives, dissenting arguments or humorous asides, the human voice is typically open, natural, uncontrived.**

Another example is the tale aimed at managers. If you want to grab their attention with a new way of doing something, prove that it will save them time, money and poor decisions, with examples that they can relate to, and that are convincing.

It's really a matter of telling it like you would tell me, sat next to me on a train. You wouldn't bother with a pompous and vacuous quote from a faceless executive, you'd give me examples of what it means for people's lives. So, give anecdotes, draw implications and use words to lodge images in the readers' minds (something we look at in Chapter 12). And do it all in everyday language, with maximum clarity. Remember, most journalists skim read (they get a lot of press releases!). If you have something new to say, don't bury it in familiar phrases, or surround it with sub-clauses. Make sure it stands out, as different.

# ▶ Identifying a sign of our times

Different is all that a good story needs to be. Not all news is the biggest, the best or certain to disrupt our drive to work. There is a class of story that makes it into the news anyway, known as the 'Hey Doris' tale. These are the titbits of dinner party talk, the oddities that people regale each other with during long walks in the country, or the snippets that get stored away somewhere at the back of the mind as a sign of our times. Almost all of these stories sell because they capture some essence of our pages in history.

Take the tale of ears grown on the back of mice, or Americans who only walk a mile a month, or the rise of a psychological syndrome as new millionaires struggle to come to terms with their wealth. These stories can look backwards, or forwards, but they are always both surprising *and* something we almost knew already.

Once television, radio, the press or the internet pick up on a Hey Doris tale, it gets front-page coverage. So, if you think you have a Hey Doris, make sure it stacks up that way. Include the telling details, and get to them quickly. In the following press release a writer has understood that the way to breathe life into this low-grade story is by capturing the sense of a moment of industrial history, but he has not applied this news judgement to the ordering or contents of the release. See what you think.

Date: Thursday, October 14, 1999 4:23 PM

## Boeing completes last Classic 737 fuselage

Wichita, Kan., Oct. 14, 1999 – The Boeing Company today marked the completion of its last Classic 737 fuselage with a ceremony attended by several hundred employees and retirees who worked on the program during the last 34 years.

'Today is a historic day as we pause to honor and thank Boeing workers for their contributions in building the all-time, best-selling commercial airplane,' said Jeff Turner, Boeing Wichita vice president and general manager. 'While we reflect on the passage into history of a truly great airplane, we also look ahead to the Next-Generation family of airplanes - the Classic 737's successor - as it takes us into the next century of flight and sets new records of performance, reliability and popularity,' he said.

Designed to replace the Boeing 727, the first 737 airplane, a 737-100, was delivered to Lufthansa on Dec. 28, 1967. The fuselage sections being rolled out today are for a 737-400 airplane model. The airplane will be delivered to Czech Airways in February 2000.

Boeing Wichita's involvement in the 737 Program dates back to 1965, when workers began building portions of the airplane's tail. Wichita's role gradually expanded to production of the fuselage of the Classic and Next-Generation 737 airplanes.

Today, Boeing Wichita supplies engine struts and nacelles, vertical fin and horizontal stabilizer, inboard and outboard flaps, and front and rear wing spars for the Next-Generation 737 family of airplanes.

There are about 357,000 parts held together by about 600,000 bolts and rivets in the 737-300/-400/-500 models. For the 1,986 Boeing 737-300/-400/-500 airplane models produced, this equals about 1,191,600,000 bolts and rivets.

The Classic 737 fuselage rolled out today will be sent by rail to the company's Renton, Wash., factory, where the fuselage sections will be joined in final assembly. In contrast, Next-Generation fuselage sections are joined in Wichita into a single piece prior to shipping.

Boeing Wichita estimates that over the life of the Classic 737 Program, more than 50,000 employees have been involved in producing the airplanes. Currently there are about 2,500 people assigned to the Next-Generation 737 Program in Wichita. The Next-Generation family of airplanes includes the 737-600/-700/-800/-900 and Boeing Business Jet.

Contact: Fred

For my money, the last three paragraphs of this are the only ones that hold any interest. This story is about our old world disappearing. Thousands of men and women spent their lives building these planes, and now it's all over. Boeing is moving on and its star performer is heading for the museum. Extraordinarily, we all know this plane as a norm of our lives: it arrived with the Ford Cortina and is only going out with the WAP telephone. Where is that first Lufthansa plane now? I'd use a Cameo on that one plane as my pay-off, after telling the tale of a great plane, the airlines that bought it, the quirks it was famous for, and how the Wichita plant was then, and is now. That way we get the obituary that this story could and should be.

So there you are, you've dropped the technical and conceptual blinds. You've found a real story, for a real audience, and made it real. You're writing stories like a human being. There's only one more thing to do: go read some more press releases: www.prnet.co.uk is as good a place as any to find some. And once you've really seen, in the full mix, what the journalists see, you may never write a press release we howl about again.

## Reading between the lines

Flip the coin and we turn from press release writer to press release reader. You must be wondering by now how to turn the worst as well as the best of press releases into stories. How do you distinguish between a badly written release and a non-event? And how do you spot the story the company isn't even aware it's offering?

First step: get in touch with your eyebrows. We writers skim read. We race across copy with an eye for the hook. The hook is our way in, and our readers' way in, to a story that works. You'll know you've hit it when a phrase lifts your eyebrow a touch, or furrows your brow, or leaves you with the slightest feeling of a question mark. Don't underestimate this most subtle of clues. The news judgement buried in the back of your brain is a more powerful pointer than any amount of logic. If your eyebrows go, there's a story that needs explaining: a veil that's down, a claim that's nonsensical (in which case, ask why), a picture that's vivid, or an element that's new to you. And new to you is good enough. You work in this field: if it's new to you, it's going to be new to a lot of readers too.

> The news judgement buried in the back of your brain is a more powerful pointer than any amount of logic.

Sometimes the hook is deliberately buried, delivered as half a sentence that points up a news story without giving it – it's almost a compulsory exercise for companies on results day. There are many subjects companies don't want to be later accused of having hidden, but which they would rather not talk about – so sensitive areas are raced over, as a throwaway line, without further explanation and often in as obscure a manner as possible. To be kind, there is also the problem of being too close to the company to be able to distinguish the elements that matter – so they are buried along with the rest.

In addition, there is an aversion to imagery that draws on human lives. Yet stories are built around readers, their lives, and the lives of other human beings. Take the Boeing example above. For me, the hook was the more than one billion rivets. After skating over almost the whole press release in a state of suspended boredom, that one number stopped me dead. More than a billion rivets! Suddenly I have a picture of 30 years of industry, and then I know where to go with the story.

So, tune in to your own sense of imagery, and your curiosity, and you'll get most of the stories going. That said, the worst press releases are those written as if we're all insiders. These you can read from top to bottom without a meaningful statement ever reaching your brain: it's double-Dutch. This wouldn't matter if the novelty of an event, or its impact on others or within the industry were spelled out: but in this kind of release, context is, apparently, forbidden territory.

There are no solutions. There is simply not the time on this planet to investigate the significance of every one of these specialist releases. If you did have time for a phone call 'is this really new?' and 'will it affect anyone?' would elicit the perspective you need to judge the merits of an announcement. But most of these phone calls would only serve to confirm a dead end, *and leave you with less time to cover the stories that are accessible*. Without a hook, a mite of context, or any inherent interest on your part, press releases that are unjudgeable must be relinquished unjudged – into the bin! You really don't have a choice about this. You do, after all, have a job to do.

Fortunately, or journalists might end up going insane, a small fraction of press releases relate to stories that are obviously worth writing about. So, now we turn to what happens once you've spotted a story and the taper is lit.

## Getting the extras

A press release arrives on your desk: it's a goodie. The deal struck between the world's largest chemicals company and one of the biggest venture capital funds, for the sale of a German paint company into US ownership, has collapsed. The press release is delicately phrased. The deal is most

## The company said ...

An in-house press officer is a spokesman for the company. The way in which journalists cite press officers varies around the world. In the USA, the press officer will be quoted by name and job title. In the UK, journalists will cite 'a spokesman' or even the company: 'the company said'. Either way, a press officer can be held accountable.

But an external PR agent is not a spokesman, and although he may be far more helpful – his mission in life being to satisfy the journalist as well as his client – he is a 'soft' source. If the information is vital, or sensitive, seek a second source.

definitely off, but it doesn't say why the deal folded and where the breakdown leaves the chemicals group, let alone the fund. The story will certainly win news space, but not as it is.

With your sights set, the chase begins. Few business stories that start with a press release stand up without more besides. And as you move to step two, there's some etiquette you really need to know about.

First to the boring mechanics: press releases are issued either by a company's own press office, or by an external PR agency (see box). Agency releases are often clearer and fuller, but both types will normally contain three elements: the announcement, or news as the company sees it; the editors' notes, which give context and background information; and a contact name and telephone number for queries. For in-house releases, the contact will usually be the press officer who prepared the release. For agency releases, there will often be at least two contacts, one within the PR agency and others at a senior management level within the company or companies involved, and sometimes even at their merchant bank. Having more contacts is far more useful for journalists, who can speak directly to someone senior and knowledgeable within the company, but also seek the assistance of the PR manager in tracking down background information or other executives.

Usually, press releases are followed up by phone, but in a minority of cases there will be an accompanying press conference, and executives will be available for face-to-face interviews at its fringes. It's when you get to the interviews – by phone or not – that things start to get interesting, because you're after the hymn sheet. Behind every sensitive press release is a hidden element: a supplementary list of further questions and answers (to which everyone you interview will sing). Producing these supplementaries is close to universal, but you will hardly ever see one: they're too sensitive!

You will, however, be able to get some of what's on there, by asking the right questions.

---

### The secret ingredients of the press officer's hymn sheet

1  **The timetable**: a schedule for the press officer or executive presenting the announcement, covering interviews for the wires, radio and TV, analysts, the press and commentators. *Category: very dull.*

2  **Key messages**: up to five sound bite quotes putting the company's case in areas where they are likely to draw fire. *Category: moderately interesting.*

3  **Questions and answers**: the 20 nastiest questions that the company is likely to be asked, generally concentrated around greed, sloth or corruption, but including any area of sensitivity, notably plant closures, job cuts, product safety and executives' own career plans. For each question there will be pre-prepared answers. For some questions further and more detailed answers will have been prepared for using 'off-the-record', that is, on a non-attributable basis, with trusted journalists. However, others will be marked as not for discussion under any circumstances, perhaps even as 'refer to lawyer'. *Category: extremely interesting.*

4  **Context**: relevant information about the industry or competitors. *Category: interesting.*

5  **Cuttings**: reports on preceding announcements. *Category: barely interesting.*

6  **Brief on journalists**: notes on the capabilities and trustworthiness of the key interviewers that executives will speak to. These may include annotated cuttings highlighting how they wrote last time and any past errors of fact. *Category: sheer voyeurism.*

---

The box above is the full whammy as hymn sheets go. It is the kind of brief that would accompany the announcement of an acquisition or merger, or something particularly sensitive like an unfavorable ruling from the competition authorities. However, key messages, questions and answers and often the context will have been prepared for even the most minor of corporate press releases. Generally, it is in the company's interest to ensure that you get the key messages, and it is in your interest to ensure that you come away with the Q&As and the context. This is rarely a pushover.

For the press officer, the whole point of the hymn sheet is to cover himself against difficult questions. The psychology is similar to the nursing of a horde of food supplies in a nuclear bunker. You won't get the Q&As just by asking what's there, or even by asking a few general sweep questions. You have to chase hard after the sensitive topics to get even the prepared explanations. Similarly with context, it's definitely a case of don't ask, don't get.

Moreover, to spice the chase, many press officers and executives will *only* answer questions covered by the hymn sheet – if your interests lie elsewhere, forget it. Pity, then, the foreign or specialist journalist. On any announcement day, there will always be journalists seeking an element of special relevance to their own audience. But the Japanese journalist's question about the implications for the Osaka plant, addressed to a company headquartered in Frankfurt, is as doomed to failure as the Spanish journalist's question to a British company about a marketing problem in Barcelona. The press officer or chief executive will not have boned up on the way in which the freshly unveiled shake-up will affect the company's development programme for engineering plastics, or its property portfolio in Newcastle. It should be possible to track down the answers to specialist questions, even on the day, and the very best PR operations will promptly set up a telephone interview to provide answers. But most companies do not have the very best PR operations.

That said, any that are better than average will ensure that you leave with a chunk of the hymn sheet in your swag bag. With this achieved, you are finished with the press release, but possibly not with the press officer. Fortunately, the reluctance of even the most recalcitrant press officer to shower the journalist with information is rarely reflected in the attitudes of the managers who are actually running a business. Again, there are exceptions, people who in any walk of life would play their cards close to their chests. There are also some companies, as we have discussed, where the control over information is so strict that any employee risks losing his job by talking to a journalist. But in the main, when asked to explain a subject that they are extremely close to, people will offer as much information as they can. The key for journalists who are seeking to make their research time as effective as possible is to identify the individual within a situation who really knows the subject.

> **Searching for a middle-ranking business source is often a winner.**

Searching for a middle-ranking business source is often a winner. Quite apart from anything else, you are likely to end up talking to someone who is not singing to the hymn sheet, which can make for some real, meaningful communication. You will also get a more personal account, with more anecdotes and much more human interest. The press officer may sometimes help you find the right business manager. You can at least get him to explain the structure of the company sufficiently that you know where to start looking. If the press release is a set of company results, and there is a mention of a problem with French hosiery, find out whether this business is managed as part of the French operation, or as part of the hosiery division. Is the business run along product lines, so that one manager would oversee both the manufacturing and customer services for hosiery, or are customer services separate? It should only take a minute or two to establish the right place to head for.

If the press office is unhelpful even at this level, you can try to get a thumbnail sketch from any existing contacts within the group, or, if all else fails, try ringing the main switchboard, and saying you want to speak to the sales manager for French hosiery. Make up the job title, most switchboards will normally find someone for you to talk to. Even last-resort cold calls will normally deliver someone in the right area within four or five links.

So, with the press release digested, the hymn sheet extracted and a real contact name in your hand, you are now ready to leave the press office behind.

**'A moment's insight is sometimes worth a life's experience'**

Oliver Wendell Holmes

# 9

# Fieldwork

## ▶ The breath of life

In geology at school, I recall scratching rocks, dropping chemicals on them with pipettes and agonizing over whether they were porous, or metamorphosed by great heats. But it was the field trip – when we witnessed cliffs twisted and warped by massive forces, dripping, echoing, limestone caverns, and corries carved out by glaciers thousands of years before us – that filled me with wonder.

> **It's inevitable in our information age that we learn most things sat at our desks.**

Artifacts are only interesting insofar as they communicate a breath of another life, or life in another time. Stand below the grand skeleton of a dinosaur in a museum and we may pause for a moment to absorb its enormity: but witness, through computer graphics, images of dinosaurs roving our planet millennia ago, and we're gripped for hours.

Business stories too need the breath of life. It's inevitable in our information age that we learn most things sat at our desks. But for our copy to be more than old stones and old bones, we have got to get out. When we meet people, we log expressions and body language, we see the working environments they've created and we get the smells, sounds, atmospheres and nuance. In the field, real things reach out and grab our attention, things that people just don't tell us on the phone. So here are a few thoughts on making fieldwork work for you, and for your readers.

# ▶ Face to face

There isn't a journalist who hasn't at some time or another put down the phone, or walked out of an office, only to be struck, within seconds, by the only truly important question they should have asked. An interview is not a passive act of reception. And getting the most that you can takes more than rampant curiosity and quick thinking – although both help.

First base is preparing yourself so you're not starting from behind. There's no way you can get as far as quickly if you begin with a blank. So, do a little swotting. If it's a company, run the ten-minute check of the annual report (see box) and scour the cuttings. Call an analyst and quiz him on the main issues for the company, and the questions he would like to see answered. And find out a little about your interviewee. Most press offices (or secretaries) can provide a biography. Run an internet search if you've time and ask the press office, your own colleagues and analysts how this person interviews – are they defensive or open? Do they respond well to teasing, logic or appeals for help?

> ### Swotting from the annual report
>
> ◆ What does the company do and where? If the annual report is unclear get the press office to explain *before* the interview.
>
> ◆ Look at the 5- or 10-year history of sales and profits, checking for dips in growth.
>
> ◆ Check the **profit and loss** account and the **balance sheet** for a low return on sales or return on capital employed, and for too much or too little debt (see Chapter 10).
>
> ◆ Look at the breakdown of sales and profits by business and region. Which are the below average performers, and which the strongest operations?
>
> ◆ Read the **notes to the accounts** on provisions, for pointers on pending court cases, environmental liabilities and any other nasties.

Then: *get there on time*! Journalists are notoriously bad timekeepers. An interview in half the time with an irate executive is no way to get the best. Once there, your first mission is to establish a rapport. No matter how fashionable the hard-hitting question with the macho school of journalism, the truth is you get more insight from someone who sees you as sympathetic. So start where the executive feels comfortable, even proud, and let him lead for a while. Only then do you steer onto more interesting ground, opening even the juicier matters with the routine and well documented.

© Roger Beale

**When you're heading for the sensitive, or even ground-breaking, go gently.**

When you're heading for the sensitive, or even ground-breaking, go gently. Move in from the wings and roll around the subject a little. If he sidesteps, come back more directly, but still calmly, slowly and clearly. And keep biting at it, until you are happy with the answer. If there is to be no answer, establish that the subject is indeed out of bounds. A 'no comment' is better than a 'reluctant to discuss'. But a comment is better still.

Often, the way to get that comment is to move off the record. This doesn't mean you can't record what is said, it means you can't *attribute* it to your informant. It's often the case that an executive wants there to be a public explanation, but he doesn't want to be credited with giving it. This may be because he's hand-picking journalists to tell – opting for those he trusts to 'get the message right'. To do this, companies must go off the record because they can't be seen to be refusing to answer one journalist, and explaining to another. Or an executive may not wish to be quoted because he doesn't want to antagonize competitors, customers or partners. Take the collapsed paint company deal mentioned in the last chapter. Both parties might want to expose the reasons for the breakdown, but neither will want to be revealed as the source for the explanation – it's like telling tales in school. Discretion is a diplomatic public posture. But it can be distinctly advantageous to get something sticky explained to the satisfaction of shareholders.

An interviewing strategy that first builds trust is likely to help in drawing off-the-record explanations. But it cannot always deliver productive interviews. Occasionally, you will encounter an unbiddably hostile interviewee, who blocks you at every turn, and never warms to his subject. Humour can resolve this, and works more often than it fails. Be charming. Smile. Make eye contact. And tease: 'I'm sure this is something you'd like to say lots about,' delivered with an impish grin ahead of a fearsomely awful question, usually breaks the ice. They will laugh. Once they have laughed, you are through to some contact, and they are left working out how much they are going to tell you now they've acknowledged they don't want to tell you anything.

Finally, there is the irretrievable interview. You may have put a foot wrong, been too direct for your interviewee's temperament, too frivolous, or too intense. Alternatively, he may never have had the slightest intention of saying a single thing of substance. Take a deep breath, smile, try again, and if several tries later you are getting nowhere, give up: he is wasting your time. Bring the interview to a close, get your information from someone else, or somewhere else, and if it is relevant to the company or its tale, address the problem of your executive's intractability in the write-up. Be sparing in this. This is not a matter of venting your personal frustration. However, if an executive is playing power games, where he should be selling the company's case, readers have a right to know – since this will be affecting attitudes towards a company across a wide spectrum. Indeed, where you have had a very hard interview, it is worth finding out what the analysts think. A common journalists' code for an obstructive and even hostile executive is to say he is perceived in the City as 'a poor communicator'. And if he really was 'reluctant to talk about the company's performance, plans and strategy', say so.

Mind, even the most time-wasting interview *can* come good. I once flew from the UK to Germany for an interview with an executive who froze me out completely – and his press office had sought the interview! Fortunately, a team of bankers sat behind me on the way there, lengthily agreeing their pitch for the day. They were on their way to see the same company, BASF, to propose a way for it to buy back 10 per cent of its shares from its shareholders. After my failed interview, I set about trying to discover if they were one of many such teams, which they were. Put together with an interview with a different, but nameless BASF executive, and a helpful analyst, I got my story: 'Banks eye BASF buy-back', as page lead.

At the other end of the scale, you will occasionally interview someone who is offering so much you are losing material through overload. Just make sure you don't lose it all. Such people have minds like telephone exchanges. The volume of traffic is huge, but everything hurtles through at high speed. You need to focus the flow. Delve into just two or three areas, and push the rest to one side. You need to use notes for this. The aim is to free your mind, so jot it and forget it. You'll end up with a list of discarded topics as a tempter for another day, and in the meantime you can concentrate on pinning down the stuff you want to get now.

## Getting a record of what's said

The greatest peril of any interview is the denial that follows your write-up, either because you got it wrong, or they did, which makes the way you record interviews critical to your future. You can't rely on your memory when reporting statements and information that will affect people's lives: even geniuses suffer memory distortion! But you equally don't want to end up stopping the interview in its tracks, because your short-hand can't take the pace.

The average interview lasts for approximately 20 minutes and, for face-to-face interviews, an hour is more normal. Recording three words a second for 3,600 consecutive seconds, whilst also running ahead with questions that prompt productive answers AND being alert to the hint of new issues, is a tall order by any count, which is why most journalists compromise and take notes as edited highlights, from which they can later pluck the critical quote at speed. This does require that your news judgement is bang on – where you don't take notes, you won't have quotes, which isn't going to go down a treat if one of the gaps is the angle your news editor wants to lead on. You can resolve this to some extent by jotting down keywords for everything that is covered. 'US market. Flat. Overstocking' will be enough to pursue this avenue later with the press office.

> Selective note-taking also reveals what you regard as irrelevant, which can rankle, and even silence an interviewee.

Selective note-taking also reveals what you regard as irrelevant, which can rankle, and even silence an interviewee. So take notes through arcane material if it seems helpful.

You can also make your notes work better for you by marking word-for-word quotes with quote marks, so you can paraphrase other sentiments or facts without confusing your summary with the interviewee's verbatim statements. I also star and box notes of off-the-record conversations. And if the conversation takes off in another, but interesting direction, leaving a question unanswered, I fold a page corner, to return to my original question at the end of the interview. Often, it will have been answered by then, but a quick check of folded corners has frequently given me material that I needed and might otherwise have left without. I also tend to start each interview with a single page of keyword prompts for questions – I fold the page at half height so that I can flick back to it if momentum slows or I lose my train of thought.

However, while edited notes enable you to get more and better stories during an interview, they also increase your vulnerability should a dispute ensue over what was said. In these cases, only a tape recording will cover you. Unfortunately, you often cannot predict these situations. Sometimes an executive will warm to a subject because he is excited about it. To you, the ground will feel safe, precisely because he is saying so much. But with the news story before him, or an apoplectic press office on the phone, he may find it politic to retract. At other times, a complaint will be part of an agenda completely unrelated to the journalist.

The only way to cover yourself against all such disputes is to tape everything. However, this needs to be in addition to notes, unless you have a great deal of time on your hands *and* a beneficent employer. Finding quotes and information on a tape-recording is a tortuous process. It can take another hour of playing back just to find your sound bites! Journalists rarely have this kind of time at their disposal. Most carry out several interviews a day as well as other research and a good deal of writing up.

| Notes ... | ... or tapes? |
|---|---|
| ◆ make the retrieving of quotes for your story quick and efficient; | ◆ free your hands and your mind for the interview; |
| ◆ are cheap and easy to store for future reference; | ◆ may capture an important aside or fact that you missed in the flow; |
| ◆ can distract you from the sense and implications of the conversation, and even inhibit its development as you scurry to record what has been said; | ◆ offer you complete cover against any dispute over what was said; |
| ◆ reveal what you expect to use in your story; | ◆ give nothing away about your main areas of interest; |
| ◆ limit the information you can use to the notes you have; | ◆ can make interviewees nervous; |
| | ◆ make retrieval very time consuming – it can take an hour of playing back to retrieve three quotes and a number! |
| ◆ can leave you open to complaints of error. | ◆ are expensive, bulky and inefficient to keep. |

Moreover, if you only use a tape recorder, you will be bound to keep every tape for as long as the statute of limitation on legal action requires – six years in the UK. At which point, if no one has complained, denied, sued or acted in some other way, they lose the right to do so. This makes for a monumental bank of tapes, and depends on your employer's willingness to afford you the space and budget for such electronic insurance. For most of us, most of the time, notes are for doing the job, and tapes are for insurance.

> If you only use a tape recorder, you will be bound to keep every tape for as long as the statute of limitation on legal action requires.

The judgement call comes when you get a good story, but the conversation has gone unrecorded. You should try for a second source or independent confirmation. If that's not possible, you need to judge the likelihood, and importance, of a dishonest retraction. As a rule of thumb, it tends to be the executives of small companies, unused to dealing with the press, and of defensive companies undergoing morale-damaging difficulties, that retract. Executives from big, successful companies usually know exactly what they are saying, and why.

That said, the only time I misjudged a poorly recorded conversation – conducted whilst walking upstairs between a press conference and a press reception – was with the executive of a large and successful company. It was not a court case issue, but the company's subsequent apologies to myself and my other team members for the dishonest denial were scant comfort in the face of a ruling by the editor that the error was mine. Unfortunately for journalists, the indiscreet and excitable executive inadequately contained by his press office is too common for comfort. You need to be able to spot the type, and mark them as 'only on tape or with witnesses'. And witnesses are what a press conference gives you.

## ▶ Working with the pack

As a rule, press conferences open with a formal, scripted presentation by one or more senior executives, and then move on to an open question and answer session. This Q&A session is one of the most productive sources of news there is, precisely because it combines access and control over the questions with witnesses. When companies seek to sidestep questions in these circumstances, journalists will normally work as a pack to get to an answer. But what you get from a press conference is influenced by several other factors too.

### Alone or together?

If you're alone in having spotted a strong news angle you'll want to quiz an executive in private to nail your scoop. You should get a chance for this immediately after the conference, or during the press reception that normally follows. But for sensitive subjects, it's often worth sacrificing the scoop, to get the witnesses. You do stand the chance of getting off-the-record material by going private. But a question in an open conference forces companies to say *something* or clearly label the subject as No Go. And no company wants to label anything as out of bounds publicly, unless it really must.

In weighing whether or not to go it alone, you also need to consider the degree and frequency with which you want your stories to differ from everyone else's. Reading your competitor's copy later, your news editor may be more worried than delighted that your story stands out from the pack. Does he trust you to have got a better story? Or will he suspect you of missing the point if you shy away from the emphasis selected by the press office?

In fact, the writers covering any particular subject will frequently be the best of friends. They share all the personality traits that attract people to reporting, an interest in the same subject area, and many common trials and challenges: of course they get on. And when it is hard to find a news angle at all, or there is a confusion of trivia, they often do put their heads together to agree a line. There are few other situations that produce a set of news stories all alike. Unless the matter has been rolled around by all, there will inevitably be variations in the information gathered and, more importantly, the emphasis adopted.

## Playing eye witness

Press conferences are live performances and the Q&A is *ad hoc* too, which means you get body language, expressions and hesitations, all as extra bonuses. But beware, body language is dangerous ground. I've heard journalists and non-journalists alike speaking with great confidence about Alan Greenspan's interest rate intentions (Chairman of the US Federal Reserve Board), or an acquisition in the offing, based on screwed-up eyes or a momentary pause. In fact, life isn't that easy. Of course a hesitation by an otherwise effusive executive means that he is searching for words. This *is* often because he is about to be 'economical with the truth' – he is searching for a way around. But it can also be because he has momentarily forgotten the relevant statistics, or because he had a conversation on just this subject yesterday, which pops into his mind as he is opening his mouth. Similarly with body language, we don't all use the same body language! While some people have an astonishing capacity to control the physical giveaways of a lie, others give the giveaways even when they're being honest, thanks to a long-standing and otherwise hidden guilt complex.

> You can forget about approaching body language with your Desmond Morris dictionary in hand.

So you can forget about approaching body language with your Desmond Morris dictionary in hand. The only time it's likely to be meaningful is when a mismatch strikes you instinctively. If you have to think about it, forget it as a clue. Do you think Louise Woodward innocent, or not? I wouldn't want to stake my reputation on it, either way.

However, at a news conference with the pharmaceuticals group Zeneca in early 1995, I was amazed when the company's chief executive was asked an entirely predictable question on whether Zeneca was, or had been, inter-ested in acquiring rival Wellcome, which had just been bid for by Glaxo. The executive refused to be drawn. Of itself this did not suggest Zeneca was interested. Indeed, until that moment I had believed it was not. But instantly I knew Zeneca was involved – his body language simply declared it. This didn't seem logical, and I hadn't been looking for it. In fact, subse-quently, I was passed copies of correspondence between Zeneca and Wellcome, and Zeneca had indeed been trying to set up a partnership with Wellcome, and was still trying to do so at the time of that press conference. If you are faced with instinctive certainty, it is not enough to furnish a news story, but it should be enough to prompt further investigation.

## The tip-off

Tip-offs are the best, and the worst, of starting points for business news stories. The best are the tip-offs borne of current or even previous fieldwork, that is from your **contacts**: people you've interviewed before, worked with on past stories, or have met at conferences, dinners, press events, or on site. These are the most frequent sources of tip-offs. 'I've just heard that six companies were raided this morning by the European commission competition people, chasing a cartel.' 'I don't know if you'd be interested in this, but there's a meeting due tomorrow and the word is the chief executive is out.' 'I was at a conference last weekend, and there's something going on, the chairman of H was supposed to be chairing the whole event, but only turned up for breakfast on Sunday, before being whisked away – it just has to be a big deal. There's no way he'd walk out on an event like that for anything less.' Tips come in all forms and sizes, but from contacts you know it's easy to establish their source and certainty, and from there to start chasing a confirmation.

> The essential element of a Drop story is that it will serve the client's interest to have it in the public domain.

Another regular source of tip-offs are the external **PR agencies**. These, however, are often about manipulation, either of events or of the degree of press coverage for an otherwise minor announcement. In the UK, PR agencies give almost all their tip-offs to the Sunday newspapers, ending the week with the thrill of the 'Friday Night Drop'. I've even heard a PR boast of climbing through an open window so that competing publications housed in the same building wouldn't twig the arrival of the Drop – though I've never quite understood why a motorbike courier wouldn't do. But then, this is sport rather than a chore.

That said, and before every chief executive thinking of turning to an external PR agency throws up his hands in horror, the Drop is about serving PR agencies' clients. There is an element of cultivating journalists – by giving the story to a favoured hack. But the essential element of a Drop story is that it will serve the client's interest to have it in the public domain. The reason it goes as a scoop to the Sunday papers is that the national dailies will then follow it up for their news-starved Monday morning editions. This ensures maximum coverage. If the drop was to a weekday paper it would be a matter of professional pride by the other papers not to follow it a day later – unless it was a gobsmackingly fantastic story, which Friday Drops rarely are.

Typically they are low-grade stories on acquisition talks, and they come the journalist's way to get a bit of premium into the share price to strengthen the negotiating hand of one of the parties. Other less common types of stories are new ventures, expansions or launches, which would not be certain of attracting thorough coverage up against the weekday newsflow. Mostly Drops are true, but a significant minority are driven by a desire to make them come true; these are not based in fact and never materialize. For the handful of journalists who specialize in Drops, the hit rate on accuracy is not to be envied.

In the world beyond journalism, the **whistleblower** is perceived as another regular and instrumental source of tip-offs. In fact, stories that start this way are a rarity. It's true that once every few months, the phone will ring, and someone you don't know will be on the other end offering a story of malpractice. But most are the detritus from some long-running dispute – the rights and wrongs are horribly confused and the broader implications are virtually nil. Others clearly amount to significant abuses of position or responsibility, but action has already been taken, limiting the story to that of an abuse addressed and resolved.

Where a case is clear-cut and ongoing, it's almost always impossible to substantiate. Malpractice stories have to be watertight. It's one thing to be told something you believe, it's another to be in a position where you could prove it was true if you ended up in court. As a result, there are many companies and individuals that journalists know far more about than they could ever print.

One way round this is to get the whistleblower to go on the record. But life is not sweet for the guy who blew the lid off the wrongdoing of others. In the UK and other countries there are now whistleblower organizations set up to protect informants from subsequent persecution. But few are willing to enter this lion's den, even with the prospect of an organization to protect them afterwards.

Finally, in among the supposed whistleblower calls are the outright hoaxes, mostly pranks. There are few news services that haven't fallen for a hoax tip-off at one time or another, but there are many journalists who have remained hoax-free. Most fakes are howlingly obvious – punned names, errors of fact and tales beyond credibility. But if you're covering all bases in establishing the truth, it'll come out somewhere along the line that this tale doesn't stack up, even when it's a fiction of more subtle flavour.

## Playing eyewitness

If you really want to know, go and see. Frankly, I hated my first few site visits. Long train journeys, smelly industrial canteens and never-ending walking tours during which I didn't have the foggiest idea what I was looking at, let alone for. It didn't stay that way. Gradually a blueprint emerged, and it dawned on me that there were very few business stories that didn't show themselves first on site. Once I knew what I was looking for, it was like picking cherries.

Manufacturing sites are, without fail, a much better source of news than most journalists realize. They reveal industry trends so recent, or so removed from the consumer and the financial world, that they have not yet been reported. It is hard to hide the impact of these current trends at the production level, although often companies can count on journalists' lack of experience. Take one press trip around Asia organized by a large French company.

The journalists, from national newspapers and specialist publications in France, Germany and England, were split into two groups for a site tour in Thailand. One group gleaned that the French company was expanding further, putting in additional storage tanks. They took this as an indicator of a thriving business. The other group learned that both of the two plants were frequently idle, one because of problems with dumping from China, and the other because of a weaker-than-expected market. The company was building new storage tanks so that it could use more of its production capacity by making different products. The key to the different stories lay on the computer screens in the control room. Control room screens are only static when nothing is being made. The second group of journalists twigged that the plants were not running, either of them, and started asking about operating rates, which were in fact exceptionally low, at less than 50 per cent. From there they quickly moved to the problems that the company was having with its markets.

Operating rates, or the proportion of time that a plant is in productive use, can vary considerably. Most site workers, when asked, will give the operating rate: it's so well-known in their daily lives few see it as potentially sensitive. Even if they do, the joy of site visits is that there are plenty of people to ask: if not about operating rates directly, then about other indicators of productivity. Any factory worker will be able to say whether the factory is run for 24 hours a day, or whether it used to be. What are the shifts? Have they changed? Do they change? Do people do much overtime?

Then there's the stock room. Before huge ecomomic trends or localized industry hiccups hit the factory floor, they will hit stock levels. Once I learned about stock rooms, I couldn't believe I'd wasted so many opportunities on previous site visits. How much stock is in there? How many days' worth of sales is it? How full does the stock room get, at its fullest? When was it at its emptiest, and how does it compare with that now? All of these things you can find out in the most roundabout piece of apparently impressed chit-chat. The point is, when sales are slow, stock rooms and dispatch bays fill up. When they get full, production is cut back. Generally, many weeks later, statistics start coming through which show that demand has fallen, and journalists report it.

If a change in stock levels doesn't say something about the economy and/or a specific industry, it will say something even more interesting about the individual company – find out why sales have slowed, or accelerated! Remember, too, that materials and part-made goods scattered around a plant are money lying idle. Efficient plants have just enough. Any kind of excess can be a sign of a badly-run factory. Site visits also allow for some real insight into the attitudes, efficiency and morale of companies, at grass-roots level. It is astonishing how differently companies approach health and safety, hierarchy and general workplace organization. Such differences can make for a far greater depth of understanding in analyzing upcoming mergers, or in identifying reasons for individual underperformance.

Finally, there is the matter of suppliers and rivals. Manufacturers buy from other companies, compete with other companies, and often sell to other companies too. At individual production sites you will garner some of the finest anecdotes going about the ways suppliers, peers and customers do business. These same plant people are worth staying in touch with. When one company I wrote about hit cashflow problems, it was customers who alerted me: suddenly the company was selling hard and cheap, where before it had been aloof and expensive.

# ▶ Ears in walls

All time is fieldwork time if you allow it to be. In airports, bankers, businessmen and analysts sit in the departure lounge, mobile phones at their ears, or chatting to colleagues, sharing their thoughts with all who are within earshot. Restaurants can be just as interesting. I was once in a restaurant in a London suburb next to a chap who was intensely excited about his work on the impending merger of two Swiss banks. He was obviously on safe ground. This was not a leak. His buddy seemed to be a very old school friend, far less successful and in a different line of work. The merger was not announced until six weeks later.

> I was once in a restaurant in a London suburb next to a chap who was intensely excited about his work on the impending merger of two Swiss banks.

Within companies, the company driver knows a lot about who's been visiting lately and a lot about the personal habits and personality of senior executives. Chat and most chat back. Similarly, if you're taking stock in a new country, taxi drivers are just great. Their state of permanently muted outrage will deliver information that none of the PR or senior business folk are going to tell you about this particular business environment.

Wherever we go, and whatever we're doing, we're seeing and hearing about businesses. If something captures our eye, it's probably going to attract a roving reader too. Eyes and ears: that's what we are. Be it the chief executive's office, or our Sunday morning run to the supermarket, we're always on the look out for the next story.

**❛** When you have mastered numbers, you will in fact no longer be reading numbers, any more than you read words when reading books. You will be reading meanings **❜**

Harold Geneen

# 10

# Accounting for companies

## ▶ Learning to read business

Accounts are the best healthcheck we ever get on companies. A business writer who cannot read them and spot the changes that matter – and need pursuing – is a business writer labouring under a great handicap. He can report hearsay, adopt postures and relay numbers he doesn't understand to readers who don't understand them, but he can't communicate about business. So, if you are new to accounts this chapter is going to take some reading, and re-reading. But be assured it's the best short cut going. And it is essential.

There is not enough here to equip you to draw up accounts. But what there is will enable you to get a sense of how a company is performing, relative to its peers, and to its own past. It will also equip you to spot significant gains, efficient and inefficient management, the first signs of problems, and lots and lots and lots of stories.

### International accounting standards

There remain significant differences in national rules on how accounts are put together and presented. But the accounts of public companies are becoming increasingly standardized, as more and more countries adopt International Accounting Standards.

For information on which countries now follow these standards, see iasc.org.uk/frame/cenl_10.htm. The main site, iasc.org.uk, also gives a great deal of information about the standards themselves, and other accounting issues.

# ▶ Profit and loss – the company budget

Money is the lifeblood of any business. How much is coming in, how much is going out, where it's being held, who it belongs to, and how assured its flow: these are the things that dictate a company's health and its continued future: the accounts tell us all these things. Unfortunately though, not in one place. The company healthcheck is like any kind of medical examination. Some things can be photographed or x-rayed in a single moment. But others we must measure over time. Like a lone heartbeat, a snapshot of the sales in one instant tells us nothing about a company's overall performance other than that it is alive.

So, we begin with an account over time, known sometimes as the profit and loss account, and sometimes as the statement of income. Essentially, this is a project of counting income in, and spending out, to leave the balance added to reserves. As such, this is the easiest account to understand, and the one most widely referred to by writers. This is a real problem. It's like thinking we can't have cancer because we're getting enough food to eat. Companies' different accounts only give us a full picture when taken together. However, in building this particular jigsaw, we shall start by looking at what we can get from the profit and loss account alone.

> **The format of the profit and loss account is almost universal.**

The format of the profit and loss account is almost universal, and starts with the total of money that came in. Sometimes called **sales**, sometimes called turnover and sometimes sales revenue, this is the money the company has received for its products, or services. It is what customers have paid. From then on, everything goes out. The first item out covers all the costs of running the company's operations. This is normally called the **cost of sales,** and will include everything from raw materials, wages and rent for premises to telephone bills, transport costs and even the decreasing value of production equipment.

> ### A word on labels
>
> The words used to describe different accounting concepts vary, even within nations. If you're familiar with the concepts, you'll find the right item. I have given only the common labels.

© Roger Beale

Accountants normally subdivide these costs into direct costs, which have to be spent to produce every item sold, and overheads, which stretch across everything that is produced. An example of an overhead is advertising. In fact, this distinction is hardly ever made in the published accounts you will see. The only reason you need to be aware of it is as an aide in nailing the culprit if costs have soared: management has more control over the overheads!

The profit and loss account then gives a sub-total of sales minus costs. This is the trading or **operating profit**. It is the amount of profit that the company has made by doing the business it does. But it still includes the money needed to pay any financial charges on loans, and taxes. Normally, these are deducted separately. First come the financial charges. If a company has money invested, this can be a positive amount, reflecting the earnings on its investment portfolio.

> ### Profit and loss
>
> + Sales
> − Cost of sales
> = Operating profit
> − Financial costs
> = Pre-tax profit
> − Tax
> = After-tax profit
> − Dividends
> = Retained earnings

But normally it is a negative reflecting the interest charges on a company's debt. With these financial charges subtracted, we arrive at the **pre-tax profit**. Then out comes tax, to give the **after-tax profit** or net income. Finally, the company distributes its profits. Some goes to shareholders, as **dividends**, and some is kept, for future investment. On the profit and loss account, the dividends are subtracted from after-tax profits, to give the **retained earnings**.

There you have it – a third of company accounting at your fingertips in one nine-number summary of what came in and what went out. Of course, in amongst this mix will be the funnies – the exceptional items that companies argue are so one-off that they should be viewed separately. Typically, exceptional items include money received for selling an entire business to another company – a disposal – or, even more common, spending on 'restructuring', which can mean anything from closing down a factory and paying hundreds of redundancy packages, to investing in some new equipment.

As a writer you certainly want to know about these one-offs, but be extremely wary of subtracting them from the grand totals for sales or profits. These totals are the facts, however peculiar some of the one-offs they include. Explain the peculiarities somewhere in your story, but don't tamper with the overall record of the last year's performance. That is the *actual* performance. And if nine numbers of actual performance feels like scant information from which to glean one, let alone many stories, read on … .

## Relating with ratios

Our first base in making sense of numbers that record performance is comparison. Is the company doing better or worse than it was doing last time we saw its accounts, and how does its performance compare with its rivals? These comparisons serve as homing devices. Where we spot changes over time, or stronger or weaker performances than rivals, we go after the reasons.

If sales have grown or shrunk, we look for the reasons for the changed levels of demand. Have new products been launched, have prices risen, has a new competitor entered the market? The company will normally mention the reasons for changes in sales, but often in a fleeting reference. You *must* get a clear picture of what has been driving sales up or down.

> If sales have grown or shrunk, we look for the reasons for the changed levels of demand.

Next we turn to profitability. To assess this, we normally calculate the **return on sales,** or **operating margin,** which is the operating profit divided by sales. This shows the percentage of sales revenue a company has left *after* its trading costs. This margin varies hugely by sector. European textile and clothing companies typically report returns on sales of 5 per cent or less, while pharmaceutical companies tend to achieve more than 30 per cent. Of course, profits alone don't tell us whether a particular business makes financial sense. Capital matters too. But for now, we are looking at profits as a first indicator of performance. Generally speaking, the operating margin does tell us how lucrative a business is. (See box overleaf.)

However, in terms of news, this information is only meaningful once we start comparing it. So, start by looking backwards. If a company's margins have slipped to 8 per cent from 11 per cent the previous year, we have a story to search for. Did the prices for its products fall? Did raw material prices rise? Were there any costly extras, like a product recall? In short, what happened to make this year less profitable?

Then look sideways, at competitors, but only include this comparison in your final story if it is telling. Average margins for the sector don't merit a mention. But if a clothing company is achieving margins of 15 per cent, in a sector where the margin average is 5 per cent, this is either a thriving operation, or there are other reasons for its enhanced profitability, which you should look for – maybe it specializes in knitting, which is almost always more lucrative than sewn clothing. More importantly, a below average margin for a sector says all is not well, regardless of whether the reason is a skew in the type of business, or just general inefficiency.

Next we check to see how well the company is bearing the cost of its debt. For this we calculate **interest cover,** by dividing operating profit by interest costs. These costs may account for all of the financial charges, or there may be other charges or even income in this total, in which case

## A word on massaging

Companies want business writers to report that they have made profits, even when they haven't, and they will do what they can to lead us that way. A common trick is to drop some of the costs to below the first sub-total of operating profits. If we glance only quickly we will assume this number is a standard operating profit. It may not be. Always check that a company hasn't separated out some of the costs and tucked them in further down, in the no-man's-land between operating profit and net income. Perhaps the most charming example of this I've come across was in Jordan, where one company stripped out managers' expenses and directors' expenses. Once these were added back into operating costs it transformed the apparent profit into a loss: which then made it appear as if it was the expenses that caused the loss! Own goal.

interest costs will normally be split out in the notes to the accounts. With the interest costs found, interest cover tells us how many times over a company could pay its interest bill with its operating profits. Some companies cover their interest payments seven or eight times over. Others are skating on thin ice, with interest cover of two or less. Interest rates *can* double. For a company with interest cover below two that means a shift into losses. Interest is a cost that it is difficult to do more than tinker with. A company could stop producing altogether, and it would still have its interest payments to meet. So, typically companies run their interest cover at between three and five.

**Dividend cover** is also worth checking, but for different reasons. Dividends are paid out of the after-tax profits, so this is where we calculate them. How many times over will the post-tax profit cover the dividend payment? Dividend cover is typically far lower than interest cover, because, by and large, dividends are within the company's control. The same leeway is not needed to cover against changes in the outside world. However, dividends do tend to be an important factor in determining the share price and if a company is already running on tight dividend cover, it may be unlikely to increase the dividend in the near future, which may dampen its share price.

However, the richest pickings from the profit and loss are not listed on the account at all, but in the **Notes to the Accounts**. These explain what is included in each number and any special circumstances, *and* they provide a large amount of supplementary information. For instance the note attached to sales will often give a breakdown of sales by type of business and by geography. From this you start to get a real picture of the company's activities.

◆ Does it sell a lot in South America, or are all its sales made in Italy?

◆ Where are its sales growing the fastest?

◆ People may call it a drugs and chemicals company, but maybe only one fifth of its sales are of drugs – the business that everyone else is writing about – and the other four-fifths are in chemicals.

◆ If there has been a sales spurt, where did it happen – was it across the board or concentrated in earth-moving equipment, and in the Middle East?

◆ Similarly for sluggish sales, have these been held back overall by a fall in sales in one particular business or area, for instance media services in Asia?

These breakdowns are filled with pointers to stories. Above all you are looking for changes that are greater than average, either up or down. Having found them, you go hunting for the story. Why has there been a sales boom in earth-moving equipment in the Middle East – is it war preparations, or perhaps a high oil price prompting the oil-rich to a building binge? Does it tell us anything about what is happening for other building equipment and materials manufacturers in the region? 'Building boom in Middle East' – get some more figures, and you have a story that goes significantly beyond this company's accounts, and provides something that could be really useful to readers.

In sum, this account tells us how sales are doing. It reveals costs that are taking a heavy toll on the company. It also tells us how profitable a company is and how much money it is returning to shareholders. However, the profit and loss account is only the summary of what has gone in and out, it says nothing about the state of the body itself. For this we take a photograph at a single moment, rather than keeping a record over time. This photograph, taken on the final day of the accounting year, is called the balance sheet.

## The balance sheet – a photo of wealth

The balance sheet tells us about the money that is tied up within a company. It is called the balance sheet because its two halves always balance. Why? Because they are showing the same thing in two different ways! The first half shows us how the money held by the company is being used, and the second half shows who it belongs to. In both breakdowns it's the same pot of money that we're looking at.

However, the idea of a company's money belonging to others is often a real sticking point in understanding company accounts. The point is that people own money and people own companies, but companies DON'T own money – they *use it*. This makes the second half of the balance sheet akin to an aerial view of a farm, with the large corn field marked 'borrowed from Sdorys Bank', and the little orchard marked, 'belongs to the Hooch family'.

So, to the top: the balance sheet normally starts by listing the places the company is holding money. These are its assets. It has **long-term assets**, such as equipment, land and buildings. It also holds a pile of current work, or **short-term assets**. These include stocks – of raw materials, finished goods, even of photocopier paper – unpaid invoices, and cash, be it in the bank account or the petty cash tin. It may also have some investments, in shares, currencies or other financial instruments.

Within this mix, unpaid invoices deserve a special mention. Companies are rarely paid immediately for the goods they sell. From the moment that goods leave the company until the moment it receives payment for them, it is effectively owed money, which is listed on the balance sheet under **debtors** or accounts receivable. With all of these assets listed, the balance sheet hits its first important sub-total: **total asset value**.

### The balance sheet

| | |
|---|---|
| + | Long-term assets |
| + | Short-term assets |
| = | Total asset value |
| − | Current liabilities |
| = | Capital employed |
| − | Long-term liabilities |
| = | Net asset value |
| − | Shareholders' funds |
| = | Zero |

It then turns to matters of ownership. First come **current liabilities**, or money available to the company on a short-term or temporary basis. This covers the company's own unpaid bills. It may be using photocopier paper that it has not yet paid for – this is effectively a loan from the person who still owns the photocopier paper. Unpaid bills are thus totalled to give the amount owed to **creditors**. Unpaid taxes or dividends are often listed separately or as sub-totals. And overdrafts and loans due for repayment within the next year (that is, over the next accounting period) are included too, since these belong to the banks.

The next sub-total is probably the most important number on the balance sheet. Total assets minus current liabilities gives us **capital employed**. Think of the logic: total assets gives us the total amount of money that the company is holding – its wealth. But some of it is extremely temporary, it will look different tomorrow, such as unpaid bills and overdrafts, so we take these out. With the temporary and rapidly oscillating stuff removed, we get a clear picture of the steady-state amount of capital that a company is holding, or employing. In fact, the pool of temporary money, and the way it is being used, is very (very) interesting to us, in terms of what it says about how well a company is being run (see box).

Finally, the balance sheet tells us about the owners of the money that the company is holding long-term. The first tranche of funds are taken under **long-term liabilities**. This is long-term borrowing, and includes loans with more than a year to run; bonds and debentures, which are notes allowing the company to borrow from individuals; and any mortgages. Of course, if you take all the company's assets and subtract all of its borrowings, both short- and long-term, the remainder must belong to

## Working capital = how capital's working

Current assets minus current liabilities is called working capital. This is the pool of temporary funds being used (locked up) by the company. **We care a lot about working capital** because it is here that we get the clearest evidence of whether a company is being well-run or not.

◆ Look for tight control of debtors. Say the accounts department is besieged, and it's taking six weeks to bill customers, that's six weeks' worth of sales revenue that's outstanding (and therefore unavailable for new production) even before the customer takes time to pay. Efficient companies bill immediately    and chase debts too.

◆ Look for tight stocks. Say the production line is inflexible, or the factory foreman and the sales manager aren't communicating, there will be large stocks of finished but unsold products, as the factory rolls out things customers don't want (locking up more money). An efficient operation will produce just what it needs to service its current and imminent orders

◆ Look for cash control. Cash is money not in productive use. If there's lots of it, there needs to be a good reason.

---

### The golden equations

Current assets − current liabilities = working capital

Long-term assets + current assets = total assets

Total assets = current liabilities + long-term loans + shareholders' funds

Total assets − current liabilities = capital employed

Long-term liabilities + shareholders' funds = capital employed

Total assets − current liabilities − long-term loans = net asset value

Net asset value = shareholders' funds

---

shareholders. This assets-minus-loans figure is called the **net asset value**, because it is the assets net of all borrowing. It always equals shareholders' funds, a breakdown of which normally appears next.

The shareholders' funds section will show all the types of shares that there are in the company plus any reserves. Reserves are profits held within the company, belonging to shareholders but not yet allocated to them. The beauty (and initial mystery) of the balance sheet is that it balances all over the place. The capital employed that showed us how assets looked once short-term debts were taken out is also the exact amount that belongs to the banks and individuals that have lent the company money long-term and to the shareholders.

The box above shows a summary of all the balances on the balance sheet.

**The balance sheet tells us about the owners of the money that the company is holding long-term.**

Don't be blinded by the jargon, think through the logic and get comfortable with them. If you're only up for two concepts out of the lot, get a good grasp on capital employed and working capital, because these are the ones we really need to know and use.

## ▶ Capital − why do we care?

The difference between income (as shown on the profit and loss account) and capital (as shown on the balance sheet) is the same for any of us. We get salaries and we have wealth. Some very wealthy people have low salaries. Others are high earners without wealth − mortgaged to the hilt. If we just looked at the earnings of the high earners, we would never predict their imminent bankruptcy. But look at their wealth too, or lack of it, and it might start to look inevitable.

All of this is true of companies. The majority of business writers examine profit and loss accounts daily, and yet never understand, or even look at, the balance sheet. They have no idea whether they are dealing with a rich company with a trickle of income, or a poor company for whom this minor income may be insufficient to meet its commitments, or stay in business. Either could be true.

The balance sheet also tells us more than how rich a company is, it gives us an invaluable set of clues to how well it is being run, as we have seen in the working capital box previously. However, the real must-have for us is a ratio put together from both the profit and loss account and the balance sheet. This single number, easy to understand and easy to calculate, tells us whether in the broadest economic terms it is worth this company being in business at all! It is called return on capital, or, in full, the **return on capital employed**.

This ratio is the point at which we relate income to wealth. The whole purpose of a company is to be productive. Its wealth is the platform it uses to be productive, that is, to earn an income. If it needs sewing machines to make clothes, it will hold a wealth of sewing machines for the sole purpose of earning an income from making clothes. Although in choosing to lock up money in sewing machines it is foregoing many other earning opportunities, so it is important to understand whether the sewing machines are generating a better income than other possible earning activities. If they are not, the wealth would be better deployed in another way.

So, to get this critical ratio, take the operating profit and divide it by the capital employed. This shows us in percentage terms how much return the company is earning on its capital. It may be 30 per cent – some companies do achieve this, and more. But what if it is 2 per cent – well, frankly, it would make more sense for everybody to take their money out of the company, and put it into an ordinary savings account at any high street bank. They would get a higher return, perhaps 3.5 per cent AND the money would then be available to be lent by the banks to more productive companies ... with the result that a greater flow of income would be generated from the same amount of wealth. In sum, everybody ends up better off. Indeed, **if return on capital was more widely understood and acted on, the consequent rise in overall wealth creation would benefit whole economies.**

The importance of this ratio makes it worth digging just a little deeper into the subtleties of the way we assess wealth. Historically, one of the main problems here has been valuation. How do you value a 10-year-old printing machine, a 3-year-old computer and a 50-year-old factory? They're clearly not worth the same as equivalent new items. So, the accountants estimate, and the way they do this is by depreciating them over time. Each year, they say these assets are worth perhaps 10 per cent less than they were the year before. They call this depreciation a cost, so it gets knocked out of operating profits. The outcome is that companies don't end up looking a lot wealthier than they really are. But there have been problems with this (see box). What if a company owns a fabulous headquarters overlooking the River Thames? On the balance sheet the building has been depreciated over many years, and looks as if it is worth virtually nothing, but in reality it's worth millions. It was this anomaly that opened the door to the asset strippers of the 1970s and 1980s. They would hunt for companies that were far wealthier than they looked, buy them, and then sell off the under-valued assets for hugely more than they had paid for the company in the first place. Nowadays, such assets are valued at fair market value to ensure against this risk.

### Boosting wealth quickly

Assets don't just get depreciated. One company I came across in Kenya had revalued its equipment as a defensive move against a feared takeover bid. The revalued equipment included a fleet of delivery trucks so elderly that few of the vehicles were by then roadworthy. This fleet was suddenly deemed to be worth more than twice as much as it had been the previous year, which made the company look wealthier, and in an economy new to balance sheets, worth more.

> Nowadays, buyers are forced to write down the overvaluation as a cost, so that it gets deducted from profits.

Similarly, in the past acquisitions and disposals had a way of distorting a company's level of wealth. When one company buys another, the amount it pays is dictated by the value it places on the income stream, rather than the value shown on the balance sheet. So a big sum of money goes out, and a new set of assets arrive, but the two don't match. Formerly, companies used to value these new assets at the amount it had paid for them, which often meant the buyer looked much wealthier than it was. Nowadays, buyers are forced to write down the overvaluation (called goodwill) as a cost, so that it gets deducted from profits. This means that the assets it has bought are valued in the new company just as they were in the old company (but the buyer takes a hard hit on its profits for the acquisition).

Finally, there is the matter of age. Say you're looking at a chemicals conglomerate. Much of its plant dates back more than 50 years, and has long since been depreciated away to virtually nothing. In terms of return on capital this makes a company look very efficient. It's producing its income on a tiny platform of wealth by running acres of inefficient and smelly old factories. If it upgraded the lot, it would *be* more efficient, and look less efficient. Of course, the old plant really is worth virtually nothing – if scrapped it would fetch a pittance. And if it's still producing good income, then it's worth running. But competitive advantage can get completely buried in this accounting exercise. Just think about what depreciation means for upgrading old capital – it's a disincentive. Which starts to give you some real insight, for example, into why British manufacturing is still using its Victorian and pre-war plants, and losing markets to the spanking new sites of its emerging competitors in Asia and other developing countries.

With all these provisos you may wonder how return on capital could be so important. But with all allowances made, we have a limited supply of capital in the world, and the desirable end point is that it should create the greatest return possible. So, you need to be aware (and communicating) this ratio for individual companies, for industries and even for entire economies. But you also need to understand what's driving the figures you're reporting, and be explaining that too.

### A word on graft and corruption

The whole point of modern accounting standards is to deliver transparent companies. The aim is that owners get the real figures and a clear summary of what is happening in their business. Corruption clearly flies in the face of this since its defining feature is that it is hidden. And it always is hidden. You cannot expect to spot bribes, fraud or embezzlement in the accounts. By the time a manager has turned criminal, he won't be producing receipts and invoices to tell us.

# ▶ Well managed, or not?

The balance sheet gives us a whole bunch of clues about the calibre of a company's management. We've already had a quick look at working capital, above, but there are several ratios that can help us further here. Any efficient well-run company keeps its working capital under firm control – this is a sum of money that can run up very quickly if a close eye is not kept on it. And then a company is using unnecessarily high amounts of capital to earn its income (indeed, if its accounts are not quickly billed and chased it's making interest-free loans to all who buy from it).

> The balance sheet gives us a whole bunch of clues about the calibre of a company's management.

So, take a look at the total for debtors. How does it compare with last year? It is amazing how often a jump in this figure is the first clue to a company becoming overstretched, or of management attention being focused elsewhere (if something's got managers so gripped they're not chasing the bills any more we want to know what it is). Obviously, a rise in debtors is not *per se* a sign of trouble. If sales have risen debtors should rise too. So work out what *proportion* of sales were unpaid for on the date that the balance sheet was drawn up – that is, debtors divided by sales. This will strip out the effects of a rapidly expanding, or even contracting business, and focus you on the efficiency issue alone. It also allows you to compare the efficiency of other companies' billing operations, regardless of the size or rate of growth of these other companies.

Similarly, take a look at creditors. If this has gone up disproportionately, the company has slowed down its payments for things. This may be a deliberate policy. Deliberate or not, it warrants an investigation. Why alienate suppliers by borrowing money for free through later and later payments if your return on capital is strongly positive and legitimate borrowing is worthwhile? It suggests a funding problem or a cash-flow problem, or both. Which again is serious stuff.

Also look at the cash in hand, and stocks, as a proportion of sales for clues about deteriorating efficiency in the use of funds. And remember, the balance sheet is drawn up on a single day in the year, the company's most public day. Any well-run company will have made supreme efforts to get these figures as low as possible in time for balance sheet day – if they are high, you can be certain that they were looking a lot worse a month earlier!

Finally, how do these figures compare with other companies in similar fields? Relatively high working capital is never a good sign, but where it is rising, as well, it is ominous.

The other big preoccupation for business news writers is a company's borrowing. In our personal lives, borrowing can be viewed as imprudent or even risky. Not so with companies. As long as a company can earn more from money by putting it into productive use than it pays for borrowing it, it makes sense to borrow. For example, if a company is paying 3 per cent on a loan, and it is earning a return in profits on that capital of 15 per cent, it's real return on capital is 12 per cent. That's a nice return that it wouldn't have earned if it hadn't borrowed. For a quick sight of how sophisticated a company's financial management is, you can also investigate the interest rates that it is paying, relative to the norm. The smarter the management, the lower the interest rates – they will have shopped around and packaged different financial instruments in order to obtain the cheapest possible loans. Similarly, if a company is carrying a lot of debt, look into the levels of risk attached to its different types of borrowing. Are there any covenants, which mean that the banks can recall their money if a company doesn't meet specific conditions? Typical covenants might be interest cover of at least two by the end of 1998. Is there any chance the company might fail to meet this covenant, and get its loans recalled?

> The other big preoccupation for business news writers is a company's borrowing.

Also look at how much leeway the company has to borrow more. Obviously excessive borrowing now will mean there is no hope of more to finance new ventures, or to cope with losses, or, more commonly, a temporary shortfall in cash. No one in the world of business precisely agrees on what constitutes an excessive level of borrowing. Generally, interest cover is the clearest indicator of a company that is coming close to the limits of its borrowing capacity.

> No one in the world of business precisely agrees on what constitutes an excessive level of borrowing.

But it can also be useful to look at gearing, which is the ratio between a company's debt and its equity, or shareholders' funds (how much it is borrowing relative to how much it is holding for its owners). In my opinion this ratio is overrated in terms of the insight it gives us. Quite often these days, when one company acquires another, its gearing rockets. Indeed, companies may end up with negative equity – instead of having a positive amount in shareholders' funds they end up with a negative amount, that is, the shares are worth less than nothing in terms of the money they represent *inside* the company.

How does this happen? It's that gap we talked about earlier between what a company's worth in assets, and what the buyer pays for it. This gap is called goodwill, and when it's deducted from that year's profits, it often creates a huge loss. This is then covered by the reserves held in the share-holders' funds, and in rare cases can all but obliterate them. This renders gearing a clumsy tool. It's useful to know whether a company has little by way of reserves left on its books, and is being funded almost totally by debt. You can also compare gearing across similar types of businesses to get a general feel for the company's attitude to risk, and its aggressiveness in pursuing its expansion plans. But there is little meaning to be drawn from fine differences in this ratio.

> **It's useful to know whether a company has little by way of reserves left on its books, and is being funded almost totally by debt.**

Finally, it's worth looking at earnings per share, which tells us what return the company is earning for shareholders. Obviously shareholders get their dividends. They also benefit from rises in the share price, according to how people rate the company, and how much they deem a share of it to be worth. But neither of these returns show us how rewarding a shareholder's investment is in terms of the amount of income it is generating within the company. To do this, we divide after-tax profits by the number of shares, to give earnings per share. This is the return on each share *within* the company. It is not the same as the dividend, which is the fraction of that return that the company chooses to pay out to the shareholders each year. Earnings per share is the *total* amount of income generated by this input of wealth. In the USA, earnings per share is considered the single most important indicator of a company's performance, whereas in the UK, pre-tax profit is taken as the headline performance gauge. On balance, I would say return on capital, as a total ratio, is more revealing than either.

# The cash statement – feast or famine

We've still got a gap. The profit and loss account checks that companies are earning enough money to keep them running. The balance sheet takes a photo of the whole, looking at what's in there. But there is one more element in our company healthcheck. A company may be earning well. It may be rich. But it could still hit serious financial problems.

The last thing we look at is cash flow. Bodies need a regular flow of food. Two weeks without, and they are in more trouble than if they had been getting slightly too little all the time. Starvation kills. Similarly, companies need cash – constantly. To be productive they need to pay workers, taxes, for raw materials, rent, telephone bills and so on. They will also have loan repayments to meet. If they have a spell with no cash coming in, they can stall on paying their bills a little. If they are not overgeared, they can even borrow money to cover their costs until the flow starts again. But there are only so many stalling devices and a big hiccup in cashflow can create very serious problems. Indeed, most of the small companies that fail do so because of a cashflow crisis. Many are profitable businesses with solid assets to their name. But they are forced to stop business anyway, once the phone is being cut off and, more significantly, once they cannot make their VAT returns to customs and excise. Late payment of VAT spells the end for a company – there is no way of stalling this bill. A company gets closed down if it does not pay.

> Late payment of VAT spells the end for a company – there is no way of stalling this bill. A company gets closed down if it does not pay.

So how do we assess cashflow? Within companies, managers run cashflow accounts, akin to budgets. These show when bills are due, and when money is coming in, in order to keep a running tab on whether there are likely to be weeks or months where there's not enough cash to pay the bills due at that time. This allows managers to put borrowing in place, or chase unpaid bills ahead of an expected problem, or increase the overdraft facility, with time to spare.

The cashflow statement in a company's annual accounts is something different again. This statement shows where there have been big lumps of spending. If a company is expanding one of its sites, the investment costs will not come evenly. There will come a point when a big lump of cash goes out – yet the phone bills must still be paid. Similarly, paying dividends takes a big sum out, as does the final repayment of a long-term loan.

So, the cashflow statement starts by giving the sum of cash that came into the business. This is after costs, so most of it will come from the operating profit, although the amount of cash a company receives will be different from the operating profit. Quite apart from anything else, the costs deducted from sales revenue as depreciation will not have involved any cash spending, so for the purposes of our cashflow statement, this amount is added back in.

The statement then totals the amount spent on new assets, like plant and equipment, before showing any rise or fall in working capital – if more cash is being locked up in stocks and unpaid bills than the previous year, it leaves less cash available to the company for other things. It then sums interest, tax and dividend payments – all money out – before summing any cash in through new shares issued. It also lists any cash that came in through selling businesses, and any cash spent on buying businesses.

Finally, it shows the impact of this cashflow on borrowing. If a company is cash negative – has spent more than came in – its net borrowings will go up. If it's cash positive – it is receiving more than it is spending – its net borrowings will go down. This summary statement – almost all of which is drawn from the other two accounts – shows us what really happened with cash. Side by side with interest and dividend cover, and the general level of indebtedness, it gives us a feel for whether cash is tight or plentiful. At the extreme that can matter a great deal. When a company runs out of cash, it heads out of business.

But more normally you would use the cashflow statement to identify what's driving a company's debt up, or down. Would its debt have climbed astronomically if it had not managed to sell off one of its businesses this year? Has it made an exceptional gain through its own investments in other companies, without which it might have looked overstretched? Is a particular expansion plan costing it dear – perhaps more than it suggested it would? The cash statement should highlight all of these possibilities.

So, with all three accounts before us, and now meaningful, we have reached the point where we should be able to pick up on most cases of company ill-health. Even a slump in staff morale, which is often evidenced by a rise in the number of days of staff sickness, or even in time-keeping, will quickly translate into falling productivity, which will show itself as reduced profit margins (as the labour costs rise as a proportion of each unit of sales income). And don't think that these numbers will always have been massaged into perfection ahead of a public outing. Yes, all accounts are creatively put together, in one way or another. But few companies can really hide a malaise. It will, and does, show itself – now that you know where to look.

> **'To understand is to perceive patterns'**

Isiah Berlin

# 11

# Delivering perspective

## ▶ Giving the full picture

Our readers read the stories we write so that they can make judgements. But making judgements from partial information is a precarious business. It involves complete trust of the person who has put the summary together. Trust that they haven't distorted or omitted key elements. Trust that they haven't overstated or understated the importance or significance of any element, or even of the whole summary. If we lose that trust, we lose our readers, which is why we use so many numbers. Numbers scale significance. It's also why we put in so much context. It is this context that turns an otherwise lone jigsaw puzzle piece into a picture that readers can interpret – with confidence.

Take the example of a company that has suffered a setback. The headline, and even the facts and figures will leave readers undecided as to whether they should pull out of the shares. It really matters what caused the problem, and it matters what's being done about it. Does it reflect weak management, or was it truly external, and in either case, is it likely to be a one-off or might the difficulties persist? How much impact is this problem likely to have anyway? Is it a serious setback, or merely a hiccup?

We satisfy these information needs with context because it allows readers to decide more, with more trust. We could simply deliver our own conclusions. But why should they trust us? We will inevitably have made assumptions with which they might take issue. We will know where the

© Roger Beale

information is patchy, or inconclusive, but they won't. That's lots and lots of trust. Personally (to make a judgement here), I don't think we warrant it.

Of course, there are times when readers might possibly be interested in *your* view of the situation: then make a comment. But first and foremost our value lies in gathering and presenting the *germane* information: and that requires disciplined and focused analytical skills. Headlines won't do it. Bald judgements won't do it. But context driven by an analytical agenda will. Which makes it the single most valuable thing we can deliver. The end-point is stories that equip readers to assess what is happening and why and how it matters.

In this chapter we look at the content in every story that relays significance. We look at the importance of numbers in providing context. We also look at the skills involved in analyzing the news and laying out the future.

# Using numbers

Numbers are our best friends and our worst enemies. As a way of capturing the weight and importance of an event, they cannot be matched: but **readers hate them**. It's impossible to emphasize enough how comprehensively and universally numbers turn readers off. Put three in the same sentence and you might as well leave a blank from there on for all the people who will still be with you, which means we have to learn to use them as any craftsman uses his tools – so that they do the job we want them to do. We need them to communicate meaning; and that means playing to their strengths.

> By using numbers to compare and contrast we can capture the scale of a problem and its impact, the degree of abnormality, and its significance in the world as a whole.

By using numbers to compare and contrast we can capture the scale of a problem and its impact, the degree of abnormality, and its significance in the world as a whole. We cannot do this as well, or as effectively with words. Big, bigger and biggest, most of the time, just won't do.

Take a story about fridge production in Mojamcoo: it doubled last year. This is our first number, and it means BIG. A doubling in something is a very significant trend. But double zero is still zero. In fact, Mojamcoo made 100 fridges this year, up from 50 the year before. World production is an annual 20 million. Here, the comparison establishes that the story is insignificant in terms of the global fridge market.

In fact, it turns out that Mojamcoo only has one plant. The doubling of production might still be great news for one factory owner, except that the plant got flooded the previous year, and had to close down for four months. So, the reason the fridge production doubled was because it fell to half its normal level the year before. And just in case there is still a nagging doubt over whether this is a growth story, we can even show just how normal this year's production level is: the Mojamcoo plant has been producing 100 fridges a year every year for 17 years, until last year. Finally, there might be one other way into this story: is the size of the Mojamcoo plant exceptional? If it is proving viable as a micro-plant where others are producing at 10 times the scale, this could be interesting as a precedent. In fact, the factory isn't even abnormal in producing 100 fridges a year. It's a small plant, but nearly a quarter of fridge plants produce an annual output of around 100.

Numbers here are tools. Simply by comparing one thing with another, in many different directions, we provide a perspective kit on this announcement. This is the only way we should ever be using numbers. Numbers are never news. Stories are news, and the more numbers can do in communicating the story the more willing we are to use them.

That's even the case with inflation – and all those other key numbers we think *are* the story. With inflation, the story is one of an economy where businesses and consumers are experiencing price rises. The number is important because it scales the phenomenon, but it is not the phenomenon. This distinction, alone, separates the very best, and most useful, business writing from the very worst. Tell me that inflation is 3 per cent, and all I walk away knowing is that inflation is 3 per cent. I have a number, but I have no insight into the inflation. Tell me a *story* about inflation, which is running at 3 per cent, and (if you tell it well enough) I walk away understanding what it means for all who are experiencing it. Which doesn't mean a legion of copy: context is about selective imagery, communicating perspective in just a frame or three. Is this particular 3 per cent important? Only to consumer good producers, it turns out, whose margins are being squeezed between wholesale price rises and consumers who won't budge on price … or whatever.

Unfortunately, our abuse of numbers goes far beyond mistaking the scale for the event. We very often report the scale without saying what we're scaling. More often still, we scale something and then leave the figure hanging with no kind of comparison to show how significant this scale is (is it huge perhaps, or tiny?).

## Hanging on to meaning

There are plenty of statisticians who apply their wizardry to businesses. Indeed, complex equations run riot through the works of many financial analysts. You don't need to be a mathematical genius in using these numbers, or even a practised manipulator of statistics. But you do have to stay in touch with their meaning. If that's not clear, or cannot be discovered, leave the number where it is, and use something else.

A classic example of this is the p/e ratio. This is such a great number, the only one we have that gives any kind of relationship between a company's share price and its business performance. It does this by showing the ratio between a share's price and the profit earned on it within the company. This makes it a scale of optimism (or the reverse). The more investors believe a company is on the rise, the higher will be the price to earnings ratio. As a snapshot, it has the potential to be far finer than 'optimistic', 'very optimistic' or any nuance thereof.

Indeed, as a number that scales optimism, it provides the most striking evidence available of a speculative bubble. Historically, a collective surge in p/e ratios has always presaged a stock market crash, or correction. So here is a number that communicates something that no other number or form of words can capture. Which is why it gets used so much.

> **A collective surge in p/e ratios has always presaged a stock market crash, or correction.**

But why don't writers explain that expectations are what is being communicated? And why is the number so often given in isolation? If I tell you that the p/e of Xtra Handy plc is 25, can you tell me whether that means investors are optimistic, or not, about this company? You can't, and neither can the reader. Instead of giving meaning to the story, the number has become the story. And the meaning has been lost. Isolated and unexplained numbers like this pop up again and again in business stories.

> **Number sins**
>
> ◆ Losing sight of their meaning.
> ◆ Using them without explanation.
> ◆ Using them without relatives.

So, why do we do it? The problem is that numbers are so valuable in saving words we can get tempted to leave out the words altogether, as we try and cram more and more meaning into every paragraph. We assume that once readers are familiar with what all these numbers mean, we can bypass the explanation. Give the number and they will know what it means. It's a fallacy.

> **Without the point, the number is pointless.**

Take that p/e ratio for Xtra Handy. The problem isn't just that the number is not explained. It is also given without any of the comparisons that would tell us what it does mean. We don't know whether 25 is good, bad or neither.

By leaving out the few words that would tell us if this share is at a discount, or a premium, to those of its competitors, we have reduced our comprehending audience to almost zero. In these circumstances, the number is only an aid to those who already know all of the other numbers that are needed to give it meaning – such as average market, sectoral or even rivals' p/es. If readers are so well informed that they have, or can look up, all the comparatives, why do they need this number in your story anyway? It's not likely that they'll have all the others, but not this one.

Even specialists don't want stories with more numbers and less meaning: because they have the numbers. And for everyone else these insider codes are a real deterrent. Nearly everyone finds numbers hard to digest, and some readers are positively repelled by them. So, use numbers to make the point, but don't make the mistake of thinking any number speaks for itself. Without the point, the number is pointless (see box on previous page).

Similarly, don't use stories to wrap words around a list of numbers. We've all seen it done: the report from the Central Bank, employment figures, national accounts or a company results story. If all that you wish – or have – to relate are the numbers, put them in a table. Numbers interspersed with 'went up by' and 'fell by' are even harder to draw the meaning from than a table.

## ▶ Giving context

The points we make in building a story *all* serve to demonstrate significance. So here's a check-list, before we move in closer. This list doesn't reflect the order in which context should appear in your story: that depends on which of these answers does the most to communicate the importance of an event and its relevance to particular readers.

- ◆ **Degree of abnormality**: how does this event compare in size, and over time, with the norm? That is, how unusual is it?

- ◆ **Relative size**: how significant is its scale in the context of its world, and the world as we know it?

- ◆ **Implications**: who and what is likely to be affected, and how?

- ◆ **The experience**: what does the situation look like now, and what does it feel like to be there – this is another way of establishing significance, by providing images readers can relate to, or identify with. This enables them to judge importance through recognition.

- ◆ **Cause**: what caused this to happen?

- ◆ **Outlook**: does the cause still exist – will this keep happening?

- ◆ **Explanation**: what do all the words, terms and concepts mean?

Delightfully, for our readers as well as us, each of these elements serve to make stories hugely more interesting, as well as clarifying their importance. Take a tale about something inherently dull: a capacity expansion. As the normal announcement – which gives the product, the quantity that will be made by the new plant and its builder – this is a topic liable to send even the most dedicated reader into a stupor. Context can, and normally will, breathe the life of a news story into it. For example:

◆ What *is* the product in question, in words I recognize?

◆ What prompted the expansion – who is buying the product and why do they want more?

◆ Who else is expanding in the same area, and where does this company fit in – will this increase its market share, or even make it a leading producer?

◆ Who are the possible beneficiaries from the expansion – new workers, consumers, shareholders, local residents?

◆ What's happening in the stock rooms until the expansion comes online – are people queuing for the product? Is there a waiting list? Have prices been affected by a shortage?

By introducing explanation, the cause, the relative importance, the implications and the experience, we've turned this announcement into a snapshot of the real world. In fact, in this case, the cause is likely to be by far the most interesting and informative element. But there's no reason why we couldn't run all of this information in little more than five paragraphs. There's also every reason why we should.

Faced daily with the driest of business announcements, it is easy to stop noticing what a parody of reality they are. The story that gives a capacity expansion as the company, the product, the amount and the builder is like the dating agency that hands out the name, the nationality, the height and the gender of a prospective partner: what it leaves out is as critical as what it puts in.

Over time, we have come to accept this as a norm of business communication. In this coded and formal form we trust announcements as real information. It looks like something that has come from a business. But this acceptance is a relic, from a time when we weren't all in business and of business. Now, we have a communications revolution on our hands, and the formal words that were once a part of maintaining a respected status are just a way of losing audiences. People need information on which they can base decisions: and in that context the four dots approach becomes irritating.

So we have to turn the dots back into a picture. To return to the company that suffered a setback: the company is Dormezvous, and the news by dots is a profit warning saying the branded clothing division has performed unexpectedly poorly in the USA, due to destocking. Here's some context:

◆ This year saw the coldest May in the USA in 22 years. Shoppers simply stayed at home and by June, with the racks full of summer stock, retailers were forced into heavy discounting.

◆ Some shop managers said they had cut prices on up to three-quarters of their summer order, typically by between 20 and 40 per cent. Normally less than a quarter of seasonal stock ends up being sold at this kind of discount.

◆ 'I reckon I'm down about 15 per cent on my summer till take,' said one retail store manager in Lexicon. 'It could take a year to make up the damage.'

◆ The summer slump in retailers' revenue forced tighter winter ordering too, which is what has affected Dormezvous. 'But we do hope to see more mid-season re-orders than normal,' said Mr Fisher, the company's marketing director. He also pointed out that Dormezvous had not lost market share. 'If anything, we're better placed than most producers, in that our clothing is weighted towards winter sales, so we should benefit more from the catch-up'.

◆ Dormezvous specializes in nightwear, with winter stock normally accounting for two-thirds of annual sales.

The two critical elements that these snippets help with are culpability, and outlook. It is really very common for companies to blame outside factors, such as the weather, the government, exchange rates and the markets, for poor performance. What we want to know is: was this a genuine case of an unavoidable and uncontrollable surprise, or does it reflect a management on its back foot?

Destocking in the USA doesn't tell me that – at least not convincingly. But the coldest May in 22 years and retailers' experiences as a result does.

Similarly, the impact on shopkeepers and the balance of Dormezvous' normal sales help me judge recovery prospects. Dormezvous is clearly flagging a pick-up this season, but from what the shopkeeper says, the remnants of this setback could linger into next year's summer ordering.

Personally, I would say these events were a shame for Dormezvous and its shareholders, and they do serve to emphasize the sensitivity of clothing producers to unseasonable weather. But on balance this looks like a short-term loss of momentum rather than any kind of structural problem: and profit warnings can mean so much more than that.

## Testing the truth

As we choose where to look for the context we give our readers, we first ask questions. But we may have already been given answers in the form of claims, and then context becomes a matter of testing the truth. When someone tells us this is the best film studio in Europe, in terms of equipment and expertise, or that growth in Latin America is set to fuel an upturn in their company's fortunes, or that the market for children's lollipops is going like a rocket, we search for evidence and counter-evidence. We're not in the game of labeling people prophets or liars. But if this film studio is the best, what does it have that others don't? And how and what is growing in Latin America? And by how much and why is the children's lollipop market growing? Indeed, when we are told anything, we look for evidence.

Similarly, we use context to test judgements. If a company is unveiling a new strategy – a merger, a new product, a push into a new market – we look for the reasons why they think this is a good idea (and any reasons why other people think it's not). We don't have to judge. We just have to collect the evidence so that our readers can.

## Analysis

Analysis is the thought process that allows us to spot what's significant, and then draw its meaning. And it starts with change. Because change is what we're explaining to our readers (that's our mission, remember). So, whether you're picking over the government's budget, port statistics, commodity prices, company accounts, industrial production figures, or whatever, it's the changes you head for. Working your way quickly to changes that matter means starting at the end-point, that is the aggregate totals. You then move back up the sub-totals, at each stage looking for more detail about the sub-total that has moved the most.

This way you won't get bogged down in the detail. The fact is the vast bulk of any set of numbers will be of no interest to you. You don't need to scan them all, and you certainly don't want a full photograph in your mind. This is just clutter. You also don't want to get side-tracked by changes that look substantial in the detailed break-down, but are of no significance in the final total. Sometimes, these make stories, and good ones at that. But stacked up against a rise or fall that's been pushing change through to the total, they come a poor second. What you're after is change that's being felt up the line.

You also want to head for the most recent figures and the shortest time-frames. For example, if you've figures for April, and figures for January to April, work from the April figures – these give you the purest sight of the recent shifts. Using a four-month total just clouds the issue by making any April event look a quarter of the size it was. Also, be very clear about the meaning of the numbers you're looking at – a rise in trade isn't good news if it's the imports that are doing all the rising, and moving the total, while exports slide. In a case like this a total of trade is a dud indicator. You need to treat imports and exports as separate totals.

Homing in on change from the totals backwards automatically establishes that a change has already had an impact. Our next step is to start assessing the impact it might still have. And we do this, initially, by looking for the cause. If the cause persists, so too will the change. If you're looking at a company, it may be the company's own actions that have marked a turn, which sends us back to strategy. If the strategy is predicated on growth in a particular market, we go and look for information on that market, independently. What we're after is evidence that more change is likely (or not). If the change is a setback, even if it's externally generated, strategy is also key. What is the company doing about it? And is the answer likely to stem the tide?

With any outside factor, what you're looking for is the imbalance, the mismatch, or the initial shift that triggered it, again in the hunt for persistence. If this change is affecting one business, look for the trail elsewhere too, because that's what will lead you to a story for an industry, nation or even the global economy.

Whatever your starting point, you need to be making the links between real businesses and big trends. Because the final element in this thumbnail analysis is the search for winners and losers. Readers want to know a fairly standard set when it comes to stories about change: where it's happening, why it's happening, whether it's going to continue, and who's going to be affected and how. But really it's the winners and losers they care about most of all. So try and get a picture of how many this is hitting, how hard, and make sure that picture lives. It's the human tale that allows recognition of the relevance (or otherwise) to the individual reader.

> Once you've got the rules off pat, you can break every single one and produce something far more brilliant.

Of course, once you've got the rules off pat, you can break every single one and produce something far more brilliant – because by then you'll have the reader so firmly perched on your shoulder you'll be answering his questions and information needs as a matter of course, which is the beauty of analysis. This is not a fixed art of putting one word or even one idea before another. It's a way of thinking which puts why in your head, and then directs your search so that you end up with what's coming. Working out what things really mean comes naturally enough to those of us who go into communicating: so just let it rip.

### A word on hyperlinks

Another way of adding value is by navigating readers to more added value. The hyperlink is one of the biggest bonuses of our new media, enabling every act of information collection and analysis to serve as many people as possible from a myriad different entry points. But it doesn't make sense if we're indiscriminating. Then, it becomes the equivalent of the search result with too many results, as readers get lost in a maze of barely relevant additions. So, get hyperlinks, add them, make the most of them: where they add!

## ▸ Making links

The why and the wherefore are powerful drivers too when applied to news judgement. By asking questions and making links, we get to the knock-on stories from the event that has just been reported.

◆ If France is suddenly taking to the internet, and the internet is predominantly in English, what's that going to do to the demand for English language teaching?

◆ If the US mutual funds have pulled out of Asia, what are they buying into instead?

◆ If e-commerce to the consumer is really on the way up, who's getting all the business delivering all those electronically ordered packages?

◆ If Dormezvous took a knock from a cold May in the USA how great a risk does weather represent for clothing retailers? How much is it affecting their performance across the industry and over time?

By making links from one story to the next, we draw the lessons from events and allow our readers to do so too. Cumulatively, this process is critical in creating a general knowledge about business and about what is happening in business. (See box on previous page.)

### A word on education

Whatever the type of information service you work for, there is likely to be scope for background briefs. These lay out and explain, in the fewest possible words (but in a conversational style), the reasons why we care about a topic, and what the inside terms mean in outsider language. As a sidebar, or easily accessible bolt-on to a whole range of stories they add huge value. They increase the possible audience, and increase the meaning that readers can draw from the news itself.

It also pushes back the barriers within our economies. We talked in Chapter 1 about collecting Kenyan interest rates. By focusing on information holes, we change the way business is understood, and thus conducted.

You should also be able looking for the value in stories as general lessons. A closely worked analysis of a cash-flow crisis at one company offers more to companies that can learn from this mistake than it does to even the shareholders and employees of the company affected.

Another key spot is the small realities that epitomize, or will fuel, the largest of debates. The different price of jeans in Sweden versus France is a story that is not pitched at jean consumers. It's a tale of our times that highlights the issues raised by the practice of differential pricing and the progress (or otherwise) of the single European market. Similarly, we need to be looking out for stories that relate theory to practice. These can be small incidents, but if they lend support, or raise questions about prevailing theoretical beliefs, they become tales that are larger than the sum of themselves.

> We are, in fact, the story tellers. We shape just as we interpret, just as we always have done.

All of these links are part of building perspective at the broadest level. We are not the academics. We are not the decision-makers. We are the people who communicate the perspective that drives the economists, the government policy-makers, the company directors and the individual in business. We are, in fact, the story tellers. We shape just as we interpret, just as we always have done.

## Building reference works

Most of the time business writers are addressing readers who are unfamiliar with the way business works. This creates a daily task of translation, from corporate speak to human-being speak, and from business insider shorthand to a longhand that's comprehensible to the outsider. This translation involves education too. Indeed, finding and keeping audiences depends on our ability to educate as we go. This doesn't mean great slabs of basic explanation. We have to nip and tuck the explanation, using a phrase here, a sentence there, to give meaning and broaden the appeal of every story we write (see box).

This, too, is context, and it is possible to do it with elegance. Indeed we need to, because a clumsy hand will drive away all who already have the picture. So, start building a mental phrase book for business comprehension. Collect

### Context to collect

- **Economic statistics**. Collect data on employment, pay, productivity, output, imports and exports in your sectors.

- **Companies**. Get annual reports. Work up a contacts list for the analysts that cover each company. Ask for a summary from company press officers of all partnerships and alliances, with sales figures or employee numbers.

- **Prices**. Find out who collects data on prices in the areas you cover and get the data on file.

- **Products**. Collect data on the market share of leading companies in different product areas, also try to get a global production figure. For some products it is worth finding out how many people own the product, especially in different countries.

- **Analysis**. Get on the mailing lists for specialist publications and journals.

smart, easy, accessible ways of explaining key business concepts and issues. It's the same art as is required to unravel any technical copy.

Finally, remember that all this scene-setting is a time-consuming endeavour. On the day, it will swallow by far the greatest part of your research time. The event of the day can be gleaned in seconds. A telephone call or two will add details. But context can swallow as much time as you throw at it.

> **Collect smart, easy, accessible ways of explaining key business concepts and issues.**

So, get ready. Whatever your area, get some reports on your shelves and in your files. You can top up all year: at conferences, site visits and during interviews. If people have background studies about the industry, get a copy, and keep it.

Build up your contacts. If you'd been writing the story about Dormezvous, you'd have got a long way in getting to the real story with a number for the US retail trade association. Contacts aren't all big buddies. Sometimes you talk to a particular specialist one time only. But have a way of reaching them, and you save yourself a bundle of on-the-day research, and make your story better than the rest as well.

**'Good writing is like a windowpane'**

George Orwell

# 12

# Finding the right words

## ▶ The need for art

Business news may once have been the technical corner, where poor writers could hang out, relaying inside-track information to insiders. But it ain't so now. Communicating business to an audience with widely different levels of knowledge, but similar needs, is as demanding a challenge for a writer as any that ever existed. It requires constant conceptual breakthroughs, a mastery of imagery and a command of the full range of the story-tellers' art.

> The better the writing, the more your readers will get from it. And if you don't do it well, someone else will.

If you think your writing is an exception – you don't believe your press release really needs to be a masterpiece of communication, or your market report an elegant piece of prose – think again. The better the writing, the more your readers will get from it. And if you don't do it well, someone else will, and it will be they who get the stories, the readers, and maybe the pay rise and promotion. Alternatively you may feed an intranet – no competition there. Except that if you render your story inaccessible, what on earth is the point of your job? If you cannot deliver information in a way that helps your readers make decisions, you can count on the axe sooner or later.

The whole value of business news lies in its usefulness. Obscure, clumsy, awkward, illogical, or overblown copy has destroyed its own value before it ever sees the light of day. It's something no one is going to keep using, let alone keep paying for. You just can't bypass the need for good writing.

Business tales must absorb and elucidate. They should be built of words that go unnoticed, because the action is with the ideas, information and imagery. These stories leave readers understanding the subject and better equipped to thrive in the world.

## ▶ Clarity, significance and force

Words about business are words that exist to communicate. If words obscure meaning, or hinder communication, they must go. **Readers invariably stop reading when they hit empty words**. Be they journalists reading press releases, or subscribers reading news, meaningless content ends your contact. So dump words that deter, rather than aid. No one wants to read marketing puff, technical jargon, clumsy phrasing or ambiguities.

Just as essentially, the significance of a story must be established at the very beginning. Vast numbers of press releases die – when they needn't – because their writers have buried the news angle. At every stage in the business news chain, a business story needs to tell the reader, quickly, why the story matters (who will be affected, why should we care, what is new here, and what broader meaning does it have?). Without this connection, business news is reduced to the so-dull-to-read you might not even be enticed if you'd been stuck in a broken-down elevator

> 66 In a 100-page newspaper, there is an average of more than 300,000 words, equivalent to three full-length novels 99
>
> Source: Canadian News Association

for the last four hours! If it matters enough to write about it, explain why. You can't expect readers to invest time ploughing through swathes of text in the mere hope that there might be some point to it all.

There has to keep being a point, from top to bottom. Each new element must follow what came before, so that the whole piece unfolds naturally, and the significance of each new point is immediately clear. Information and the reason why it matters should not take turns. Facts should be interlaced with explanation, and claims woven together with context. For, be sure, bullet-fire news, hard and fast, with no connection or context, will throw up a row of question-marks so long in your reader's mind that even the most willing will give up in bewilderment. Similarly, the jolt of an indigestible wad of explanation will lose you readers.

The key is to avoid clogging up your readers' (just seven) units of short-term memory with open query files. Address questions before they have formed in the reader's mind, or, at least, as soon as they are left hanging. And, remember, if you leave just one question prompted, but entirely ignored, it will be that thought that abides, not a sense of satisfaction at the wealth of information gleaned from your piece. And all this needs to be done in as few words as possible, as quickly as possible.

Web users keep pages open for an average of 59 seconds.[1] Newspaper readers, radio listeners and television viewers, don't give a story a much greater chance. In almost any media, you get one shot at capturing your reader's interest: and that's one shot with every line. Lose once and the reader won't be giving your story a second chance, which is where use of language matters. Writing short is not about keeping the word count down. It is about maximizing the meaning of every word.

> **Writing short is not about keeping the word count down. It is about maximizing the meaning of every word.**

The words in news need to lodge imagery in the reader's mind. When you read a well-written news story, you don't put it down thinking: golly, that was evocative! But it will have been. There will be words selected as brush strokes, to create nuance, lend weight and short cut wordy explanations (see box), which is why news editors hate clichés. Clichés use up words lodging nothing in the mind. They are dead through overuse, and as such are wasted words.

That said, you do sometimes need words that add little, just to give the reader a brief rest while you take him forward. Because readers get tired.

---

### Got the picture?

'From the day in April 1995, when he **shovelled** billions of the family fortunes out of dull old DuPont into boom-to-bust Hollywood with the purchase of 80 per cent of the former MCA group, he found it hard to shake off his reputation as an arriviste wannabe.

'The boy who made a **forgettable** film with his Dad's money at the age of 17, skipped college for showbiz, and still writes sentimental love songs under the pseudonym Junior Miles, might be indulged by his parents, but not by Hollywood.'

Extract from profile of Edgar Miles Bronfman Jr, sparked by his glory moment in folding his family's company, Seagram, into Vivendi of France, written by Christopher Parkes in the *Financial Times*, 17 June 2000

Pack too much in and the intensity of the copy will drive them off. Stories need pace. When you've introduced something complex, or vivid, ease back for a second, and allow your consumer a moment to cruise. Put it together, and your business story is, for the reader, a rewarding process of unhindered reception – not a struggle to extract sense and maintain interest. And, if all of that sounds like a lot, worry not: this is how it's done.

## Cutting out the rubbish

Marketing puff is easy to delete. These are words that inflate significance – or seek to – through associations with positive emotions. No one buys this flaky over-hype. It's just a good way of losing credibility, and irritating readers. Much more importantly, this meaningless content can end up burying the real news, sometimes without trace. And if you still need convincing on that, take a look back at the Renault press release in Chapter 8.

## Translating the jargon

Jargon makes me shiver! The opposite of communication, it keeps the masses out, and the eggheads in. Construct a language of your own, reserve it for your kind, protest at all efforts at translation, and perhaps you deserve to be misunderstood. But does everyone else deserve to misunderstand you? I don't think so. Readers about business don't often have MBAs, few have science degrees, only a minority are IT high-fliers, and many could not put together a set of FRS III company accounts if they had to. So, if you want to write in a way that excludes all but the specialists, do so at your peril. Alternatively, **translate the jargon**!

In this one area don't be scared to use more words, if more words say more. Quite often a technically correct, but specialist term, is the only way of saying it in one, so say it in five. If you don't, you have just limited your comprehending readership by as much as 100 to 1. Why do that? Were four words saved worth a 99 per cent audience loss?

In some cases there is no way to make something comprehensible without offending the technical experts. The justification for the jargon in the first place is that it is necessary to convey a precise meaning. Try to translate it and the precision inevitably suffers. Clearly one answer is to offer the translation first, and then back it up further down the story with the technical term, re-explained or not as it merits – that is, if you think your readers can stomach the technical version at all. The balance on that lies with the style of your news service.

The more adept you become at jargon translation, the less you will offend, so start a dictionary now. No one has yet put together the reference work which tells us how best to communicate terms as disparate as social linkage, GDP per capita, p/e ratio, ethylene cracker and data mining. So we have to do it ourselves. But you're not absolutely on your own. There are a few other writers out there. So, buy a notebook, and start collecting. When you see a great translation in someone else's copy, adopt it. And start creating your own. Quiz experts, be merciless. You cannot translate until you understand yourself. Once you understand, just keep working at finding the tightest, most meaningful explanation you can. The first try won't often be your final solution, but the more you do it, the better you'll get.

## Moving beyond bad habits

Clumsy phrasing, and ambiguities, are the product of a writer's mindset, or state of mind. We can't help having bad days: the most elegant writer can produce spaghetti when flu is setting in, the attic pipes have burst, or the biorhythms are hitting a triple zero. Nor does it help that we have to produce everything so quickly. Business news writers have to produce to deadlines that many other types of writers never have to target: and our subject is complex. Here, anyway, for those times when the muse is dithering, the words are scrambling and the sense is long-gone, are some pointers on making yourself clear.

> When we stop wanting people to understand what we have written, we are all capable of producing garbage.

### Choose an audience

Habitually poor writing is normally caused by nothing more significant than a disconnection from the reader. If you were explaining your story to your grandfather, college pal or best friend, some automatic communication imperatives would cut in. You would want them to understand, and so you would be finding ways of making that possible. When we stop wanting people to understand what we have written, we are all capable of producing garbage. So, choose someone you admire, and even if you don't write the story to them, at least read it for them, before you file it. I promise you, it's as handy a trick as I know of for making the incomprehensible, as well as the shamefully overblown, leap out at you. And once you can see it, you can rewrite it.

## Lean on discipline

If it's a truly bad-hair day, and thinking is not an option, just join up the dots. Better a single clear line, without depth, than a mass of scribbles.

- Keep your sentences very (very) short. If you're considering one subclause, let alone three, go for a full-stop instead.
- Limit your content. Exclude every word, idea or assertion that doesn't make obvious sense to you (even in your reduced condition).
- If necessary, be willing to write the story backwards, ordering the facts and context for further down the story before you write the top (which explains the import, and grabs the reader's eye).

If it still comes out badly, here are a few golden rules for the elimination of chronic bad writing.

## No Pulitzers here

You are not going to now, or ever, win the Pulitzer Prize for literary brilliance. If you think you are one of the world's great writers, or are seeking to be, forget it. Have fun with your writing, certainly. Enjoy it, definitely. But throw away notions of great literature. Pretension will come between you and your readers every time. If you try and have a 'style' you will muddy the water. Your style will develop anyway. But if the effort is conscious, and geared towards recognition of the brilliance involved, you will surely damage the flow of communication. When you are writing, think about how best to achieve understanding, never think about how to achieve literary brilliance.

## Less is more

Always seek to say what you want to say in as few words as possible. Most confused and confusing writing happens at length. If you say the same thing in fewer words it becomes clearer – perhaps because the act of compressing forces you to focus on what you really do want to say.

## Cluster information

Group all the information about a particular subject, or angle, together. If you cluster your information by topic, you will automatically avoid the repetition that comes with poor structure, as well as the confusion generated by split subjects and half-developed ideas.

## Personality counts

Your style as a writer will reflect your personality. If you hold back, observing, until you feel you really have something worthwhile to say, you will find it hard to open stories with a trumpet. Achieving a 'read me, I'm worth it' intro is something you will have to work at. Or if you operate on emotion, connecting passionately with every story you research, your challenge may be curbing a tendency to overblow – normally with a surfeit of adjectives. Whatever your way of operating in the world, give it a little thought and it might highlight instantly the only long-term weakness in your copy.

## Be curious

Allow yourself to be insanely curious. Ferret out everything, collect it all, get gripped, get involved, get excited. There is no chance of engaging your reader if you never become involved yourself. Get inside the subject, and you offer your readers the chance to do likewise, which feels like value in a way that an aerial photo doesn't. Don't just deliver a picture of a building: explain that there's a man in the basement sitting on a wooden stool who spends his life changing temperatures in test cabinets until 10-year-old plastic samples crack.

> **Ferret out everything, collect it all, get gripped, get involved, get excited.**

## Finally ... guard your scepticism

Scepticism is a must-have quality for a business news writer. If we received every piece of information with wide-eyed acceptance, we would be nothing but the tool of the last person we spoke to. We have to question. But don't let your doubt get out of control. When writers become so jaded they believe nothing any more, their copy reads like an old rag. It's dry, dull and disengaged. If we don't believe in the value of what we are writing, what chance is there that it will communicate its value to our readers?

## Routine maintenance

Powerful copy rests on powerful words. So, keep your copy tight – a matter of routine maintenance.

1 **Cut out redundant words**. Do you need this word? Does the sense change without it? Does it add anything? A triple No equals delete.

2 **Eliminate pretension**. If a short word will do, use it. That is, use it, not utilize it.

## Setting the pace

Pacing copy requires fine-tuning. Flow is essential to a good read. Every thought must be connected, fore and aft. We shouldn't jolt, jump or lurch into new topics. We flag, and we link. If we don't, we stall our reader. And if he doesn't pull away the first time he's brought up short, he will the third time. But the trouble is if we make it too continuous, we'll also lose him. A monotone pushes human brain waves in just one direction: towards sleep. At the extreme, a business story with the variety of pace and tone of a shipping forecast won't just stay out of the pleasure camp: it is the stuff of an afternoon nap.

Any really steady flow of words is like staring out of a train window. Initially, it's absorbing. Then the brain starts drifting – towards what to buy at the supermarket tonight, or into re-runs of recent conversations. If your reader is allowed to cruise for long enough, the back-of-his-mind query over whether it should be pizza or sandwiches for lunch will become a front-of-the-mind reason for putting down your story. So we use tricks to recapture his whole attention. We accelerate, or we halt for a momentary set piece.

To achieve a burst of speed, we cut in with a rapid spate of short sentences. Very short. We also build this bullet-fire effect around repetition (in threes). Like this. And this. And this. And then there is the halt that holds.

For this we need something just slightly – and I mean really slightly – clever. Normally we alliterate, or corrupt a cliché. The aim is to get the reader to hesitate for a split second, while he ponders the novelty of the words, but not for so long, or so thoughtfully, that his connection with the story is broken. And definitely not for long enough to wince.

We also work at eliminating repetition. Stale language lulls. It can even repel. Few words bear a second outing in the same place: as soon as they reappear they deaden your copy. You should always be reaching out for fresh words. Not long ones, or obscure ones, but sharp, apt, able words. They are more interesting. Indeed, if you are not deliberately using repetition to jump-up the pace, there is only one reason for it and that is for sense. There just are some words that are essentials, repeatedly. Like 'sales' and 'company' and 'he said'. If you score out, or rewrite, the results will be absurd. You will leave readers confused about who is speaking, or jarred by an alternative so elusive their concentration is broken. Under any other circumstances, avoid repetition.

## ▶ Using imagery

The fuel that makes the whole piece move is drama. The greatest challenge for a business writer in producing absorbing copy is bringing his subject to life. Making it meaningful and real. And for this he needs a muted drama that requires far more technical skill than the in-your-face clamour of copy built to shock.

**The greatest challenge for a business writer in producing absorbing copy is bringing his subject to life.**

At the heart of this skill lies the ability to evoke. You need to be able to say more with a single word, subclause or related detail, than you could with several hundred words of straight explanation. One of my favourite examples of this was a term coined by the then transport correspondent at *The Times* in London when reporting the axing of the overnight train service from London to Scotland. Not an obviously stimulating tale. Until he described the train as the 'Deerstalker Express'. Wow!

Evocation only works when it touches a chord. This chord is 'a world lost' and one of the reasons it works is because it operates on several levels. In fact, I'm only going to make it clumsy by spelling it out, but for the sake of the example, here goes. The deerstalker is a hat, associated by most of us

---

### Steering off cringes and winces

◆ Never (never, never) use a cliché, unless it's doctored into something with real meaning for your story.

◆ If you can't get the right word(s), then abandon the attempt altogether – better no imagery than the wrong imagery.

◆ Don't have two shots at the same scene, do it once or not at all.

◆ Never use a grander word than necessary: all the power here lies in subtlety.

---

with a bygone turn-of-the-century world, a world in which Sherlock Holmes lived – and wore a deerstalker. Overnight trains arrive very early in the morning, as the mist is rising. These arrive in Scotland, where deer are and deerstalkers go (wearing their deerstalker hats). These are people travelling into a surreal world of early light and damp moors, a world still open to all of us, but not often remembered.

At a stroke, axing the train becomes an example of another way in which the modern world is ending something we hold dear, even if it was never personally experienced. The label makes this more than a boring train service; it becomes representative of a way of life. In fact, in this case, the story took wings, the label was adopted everywhere, and the decision was reversed. Had *The Times* reporter spelt out these connections it would have looked like hype. But by just hinting at a world lost, the story became something readers cared about. Something real, and human. You can't always do this with two words. But the art lies in recognizing the essence of what you are seeking to capture. If you don't, the whole thing can misfire, horribly.

Wherever it is used, imagery should create a picture in your reader's mind. Prose that is laboured, clichéd or inappropriate, doesn't just prevent the creation of a picture, it distracts readers completely. It's simply bewildering, and suddenly it's your voice, in clumsy tone, that is obvious, and not the story. Your authority is ended and so is your reader's involvement.

When people read our stories they don't want to feel us in them. To be digested as legitimate news, the copy needs to feel bigger than the product of just another little human being. Failed imagery is mere mortality at its most obvious and cringe-making. So, if it doesn't feel great, delete it (see box above). Drama that drowns out the news is helping nobody. For me, the test of a written brush stroke is emotional. If the word makes you feel the truth, without intellectualizing it, it is the right word.

Typical might be the language used to paraphrase an executive – if he is a dynamic, no-nonsense achiever, short, powerful verbs will communicate the sense of that. A less-able manager, who leans on pompous language with little substance can similarly be passed on, by injecting some overblown management-speak into the paraphrase.

Numbers, too, should be introduced to create pictures. We have already looked at their role in truth-testing.

> ### A brush stroke too far is actionable'
>
> When a journalist writes 'he claimed", he is casting doubt. Unless he backs up the suggestion that the reported statement is inaccurate – with other information – a company can legitimately argue that its reputation has been damaged by the insertion of "he claimed"– although few would bother.

Often, numbers employed to substantiate or contradict a claim will draw on imagery in the process. Take the example of a new European registration procedure for existing, as well as new, agrochemicals. Producers were complaining it was excessively onerous. So, how can numbers help?

*'Each registration requires a dossier of up to 60,000 pages (a quarter of a tonne of paper) that takes three man years to prepare at a cost of 500,000 euros.'* These numbers go at least some way towards evoking the complexity of the registration procedure. In fact, they were collected during an interview at the sidelines of an annual results conference, and used in an *FT* story some weeks later on the forces driving consolidation in Europe's agrochemicals industry. This kind of time lag is typical. When it comes to imagery, we need to be collecting everything, all the time. As soon as your curiosity is aroused, or something seems important but you can't get a picture of it in your own mind, you need to be delving for the kind of details, and quotes and gossip and images that will later allow you to communicate to business readers at full volume and with clarity. As a business writer you need always to be receiving on all levels. Telltale details are part of our art. We take them and we hang tales on them.

## The laws of structure

The opening line of any story needs to hook the reader. It flags up the subject matter. For a news story you spell out the event and why it matters. Then give the information, grouped by subject in diminishing order of importance to the reader. For a feature or news analysis you can launch with an anecdote, image, contradiction or assertion. You then follow in the second or third paragraph with the 'nuts and bolts' paragraph, which explains what this story is going to be about. Again you work in mini-chapters, through the main issues and trends relating to your subject, but your order is dictated by the need to build a platform to your conclusion, rather than being a simple pecking order of importance.

Throughout both types of story, each statement should be woven together with the data that reveals its significance. And you should make links from one subject to the next, so that the whole thing follows a thread, rather than just seeming to leap about. The key to this linking lies in recognizing the questions that the last paragraph might have raised. Always be thinking about this. If you say market share has grown, next explain how and why, and then let that roll on into the effect on the company, and then explain those effects. Be driven by the logic of the tale. Don't say that investment has shot up, and then remember three paragraphs later to point out that debt has risen too. We don't make links, they exist and we follow them. The debt's gone up because investment spending has shot up. And if a piece of information seems relevant and newsworthy but links with nothing, then it isn't. Nothing newsworthy is a stand-alone piece of information. The world isn't built that way.

Finally, you save something telling for the closing line. A story, be it news or analysis, should not just read as if we stopped because we ran out of words. It should end with what is normally called the 'pay-off line'. A reader should feel as if the information has been put, and now here is the wrap-up: the pithy, where it all naturally ends, closing line.

## ▶ Rapid writing

The news editor is on the phone. He wants 450 words for the front page of the second section on a just-announced merger of two Japanese companies, in 50 minutes – and you have never heard of either of them, know nothing about the sector, and there are no wire stories on the subject, just a two-line announcement. This is the kind of rapid writing that we all have to do sometimes. And it has to be talked about, because the speed at which it must be put together renders a large number of the rules above impracticable! Who can mess about with imagery, when there are another 100 words to find and nothing left to say? In fact, in these circumstances, it's the research skills that make for a worthwhile story.

Recognize that 90 per cent of the time available is going to be spent gathering information, and be willing to spend several minutes working out how it will be easiest to get the most helpful possible information. If this reflective moment means you end up getting all you need from one phone call, rather than being empty-handed eight phone calls later, it will have done more for your story than any amount of writing skill.

**The relationship between a writer and an editor who share a clear understanding of what makes a great piece of copy is nearly always one of mutual appreciation.**

Your first priority is to get the announcement, however bare-boned it is. You then go for the big picture, preferably from someone who has a little instant detail to hand. For the Japanese merger, an English-speaking regional and sectoral specialist based in Hong Kong might be a pretty good starting point – but only if you have a telephone number to start with. The key is to work with what you've got already that might help. This is not a moment for primary research. You may even bypass phone calls altogether, working with the announcement and using news databases to give the context. Here, your choice of keywords will dictate how much you get that's useable, how quickly. But the kind of things you are looking for are sectoral overviews, similar recent merger announcements (is this a trend?), and information about each merger partner's recent performance.

Then you order it by how relieved you were when you got that piece of information – the biggest rush for you makes the second paragraph after the statement of the merger, and so on down the story. You just use the best possible information you can until you hit the word count. And if you've five minutes left to spare (which you probably won't have, because typically this kind of story is still 80 words shy with 53 seconds to go), you can edit it to make sure the significance of each point is drawn as fully as possible. Then file, and take five minutes off before you do the rewrite, with knobs on, for the next edition.

# Editing

A truly fine editor knows when to leave copy unedited. A poor editor edits everything. The difference between the two is that the first understands the rules of writing every bit as well as a first-class writer, but applies them from a different vantage point. A writer constructs a tale by selecting the significant from infinite options. An editor starts with a blank and tests the story for the understanding it delivers, eradicating reader turn-offs along the way. Typical are poor links, poorly grouped topics, questions raised but not answered, limp and redundant language and clumsy phrasing.

This joint construction of a story by its researcher and by an inside test-reader is the surest way of delivering a strong final product. Indeed, the relationship between a writer and an editor who share a clear under-standing of what makes a great piece of copy is nearly always one of mutual appreciation. It is a mighty task for any human brain to see everything and then construct a summary that unfolds from zero to sum without hitch. But together, editor and writer can spin purses of silk.

## Note

1   Web usage statistics from NetRatings, February 1999.
    209.249.142.16/nrpm/owa/NRpublicreports.usageweekly

---

**For information about Jenny Luesby's current programme of one-week residential courses, and customised on-site training, please see www.business-minds.com**

# Index